Alcohol, Drugs, and Family Healing

What are YOU going to do about that?

To Linda —
Peace and joy
from our home to yours —

Barbara Fredricks

- Barbara F.

Alcohol, Drugs, and Family Healing:
What Are You Going to Do About That?

Published by Wheatmark®
610 East Delano Street, Suite 104
Tucson, AZ 85705
www.wheatmark.com

ISBN-13: 978-1-58736-705-2
ISBN-10: 1-58736-705-X
Library of Congress Control Number: 2006933093

For Michael, my precious son, whose "problems" taught me life's important lessons.

For Linda, my daughter and priceless treasure, who shared her strength with me in times of greatest need.

For Bob, my husband and true partner, without whom this book and its story would not exist. Thank you for rescuing me from Room 12.

I love all of you mightily.

Contents

Foreword. vii

Introduction ix

1   How Did It Come to This?. 1

2   If Only I Could Kill This Monster ... and
    Release My Son! 6

3   Forgiveness. 9

4   The Beat Goes On 15

5   So ... How Long Has Your Son Been Drinking? 26

6   Moving in a Positive Direction. 30

7   The Big "R"—Responsibility 40

8   The Fatal "F"—Fear 47

9   The Big "D"—Detachment 53

10 Meanwhile, in Treatment 60

11   Life After Treatment 70

12   In Closing 73

Additional Materials

Addiction Progression Chart 78

Explanation of the Addiction Progression Chart 79

Study Questions for the Addiction Chart 85

Planning an Informal Intervention 89

Helpful Shortcuts 98

Self-Evaluation Questions 100

If You Choose to Attend Al-Anon 105

Helpful Twelve-Step Concepts. 108

Journaling 112

Expanded List of Characteristics of Codependency. 116

Foreword
by Bob F.

After more than thirty years of "trial and error" in learning the lessons of recovery, I am proud that this little book, born from the pain and ecstasy of the dynamics of chemical health issues, can help families move in healthier directions. For years, I thought the "problem" was the drinker or user's alone and that the family was a separate issue. Today, I believe the dynamics of the "dependent" and the family can serve as a model for any chronic illness we may encounter in life. The recovery principles outlined and simplified in this book are applicable to the challenges that life offers all of us. May the lessons of our family's journey be of help to you in yours.

Bob F.

Introduction

Immature, irresponsible behavior is an ever-increasing problem in our homes, relationships, and workplaces. It is a problem that appears to have an easily identifiable villain; but, after closer inspection, it looks more like a dance pattern with steps so well learned that the participants seem to go on for long periods of time, hypnotically repeating the same pattern over and over again.

In my home, the immature, irresponsible behavior was largely a byproduct of a family member's chemical dependency combined with everyone else's response to that chemical dependency. This is very often the case. I came to see addiction as a disease that nobody would want to contract if he/she knew the outcome and could avoid it. It spreads its life-destroying symptoms to all those in close proximity. Like it or not, the impaired person and everyone involved with him/her all end up in the same leaky boat. This story is about my son and me, but the dynamics apply to any situation or relationship where addiction is involved. All addictions have common symptoms and responses.

As a person who has lived the story you will be reading, I can give you my personal assurance that there is life on the other side of the tunnel. There is health and happiness waiting for both the impaired person and those of us who have behaved as though we were addicted to helping that person "straighten up," "get better," "meet his/her potential," and other pipe dreams. The way through the tunnel is filled with many ironies, such as:

- In order to be a winner, you have to totally give up.
- In order to have peace of mind, you only need to let go.
- In order to make everyone and everything around you better, you just need to work on yourself.

More about all of that as we go along.

This book is intended to give you a brief beginning education about the dynamics of immature, irresponsible behavior and families who are caught up in the dance of addiction. The information has come from many sources, many wonderful people who have helped me along the way and, of course, from personal experience in my own life. I hope it will be of use to you on your journey.

Blessings from our home to yours.

Barbara F.

Chapter One

How Did It Come to This?

"**I**'m a better person than you are because I forgive you for ruining my life!"

The words were surrounded by four-letter expletives and hurled at me in contempt.

"Me ruining *your* life!" I screeched at my twenty-six-year-old son, beyond being shocked by the anger I felt. Beyond being shocked that our relationship had deteriorated to this level.

Glad that my parents lived hundreds of miles away and my father, a minister, would never know what was being said in my home at that moment.

"What do you think has been happening to my life since you were fifteen years old?" I asked, in a voice breathless with hurt and frustration.

A slight smirk spread over his face as I sputtered on about the sacrifices I had made for him, how hard I'd worked, and how much love and care he'd been given. He knew I'd been hooked and reeled back into the dance.

"All that detachment stuff from those meetings you go to

is for people who don't understand anything about family," he
said. "Mom, be reasonable. I just need a place to stay while I
get back on my feet." His mood shifted from anger to righteous
indignation. "That lousy guy I worked for was so stupid. He tried
to blame every dumb thing he did on me. It's a wonder I could
stand it this long."

"Four months is a long time?" I wanted to ask sarcastically,
but, for once, I restrained myself.

"And you know all the money problems I have," he went on.
"Besides, you owe me. Didn't I help finish the carpentry work
on your new deck? And you have to admit I didn't charge you
nearly enough for all that work."

I looked at my son with a swirling mixture of tenderness and
rage. Yes, he had helped build the deck, but he was repaying one
of the loans I had made to him. And, according to my reckoning,
the work he had done didn't touch the amount of money he owed
me. There were the cash loans, the legal fees when he was in jail
for drunk driving ("Mom!" he cried into the phone. "You've *got*
to get me out of here before I get raped or killed. You should see
the kind of people who are in here with me."), the cosigned loan
on a car that he "forgot" to pay insurance premiums on. Oh, yes,
and there was the time I had put down the deposit for an apart-
ment and guaranteed his rent payments, only to receive a call
several months later telling me that I owed the landlord money
for cleaning up lobsters that were left in the freezer when the
"boys" moved out and the electricity was turned off. There were
the times he had moved back into my home after losing jobs or
making another try at college. I sometimes came home after a
long day's work to find dirty dishes on the floor in front of the

television, where he had spent the whole day instead of keeping his promise to look for a job.

When he and his first wife moved in with me because they couldn't afford a place of their own, both smoked in the house all day while I, a nonsmoker, looked for excuses to work late. Then I would sit in my car, dreading to get out once I arrived home. (Of course, both drank and used drugs, but I was still living in such a state of denial, I convinced myself that I didn't know about that.) I refereed marital and physical battles between him and his assorted wives. I drove people to the emergency room. I settled disputes when the inevitable infidelities turned apartments into battlegrounds. I loaned money for emergencies, including rent, car repairs, and utility bills. I paid the expenses when he came home to recuperate after a long hospital stay due to another drunk-driving experience, this time on a motorcycle.

Anger welled up in my throat, only to be followed by guilt. Often, at moments of the most anger, unexpectedly I'd be overwhelmed with feelings of guilt.

How had all of this happened? Where had I gone wrong as a parent? What had become of the sensitive little boy with the shy smile that always melted my heart? What had happened to all that intelligence and potential he had as a child? Wasted, everything wasted. Intelligence, time, potential, my love, care, money, all wasted. I had tried so hard to be the very best mom I could. It was hard to be a single parent. I had sacrificed so many things for myself so that my kids would feel good about themselves. I had worked hard so that my kids would feel provided for and safe. Even as they grew older, it seemed that most of my thoughts and concerns were about them rather than myself. I never stopped trying to be a good mom. I never gave up.

Anger swirled back into the mixture of feelings. It wasn't fair! Why me? I didn't deserve this kind of heartbreak. Other parents, even people who neglected or abused their kids, ended up with grown children who treated them better than this. Poor me! Had any parent ever felt so alone, so frustrated, so abused, so humiliated, so disrespected? Why me? What had I done to deserve this?

Slowly, the self-pity started to turn back into anger. If my son would just straighten up and quit drinking and using drugs, everything would be all right. How could he abuse his body, his mind, his family this way?

Notes

- What incidents in your family have left you with similar feelings?

- Describe your emotional responses to the latest problems.

Chapter Two

If Only I Could Kill This Monster …
and Release My Son!

I knew he was still in there somewhere. I knew it sounded insane, but it reminded me of that old movie about the aliens who had taken over human bodies. Something terrible had taken over my son.

"God, I hate him for what he's done to himself."

I was crying as Bob and I walked along the waterfront in San Diego, oblivious to the beauty around me or the concern of this man who cared for me and would soon be my husband. Once again, I was firmly caught up in the insanity that I could … should … HAD to save my son from himself.

If I had kept track of all the hours spent in this same emotional whirlpool, what would it have added up to? Weeks? Months? Years of my life spent in this futile emotional backwash? I could tell Bob was near the end of his patience. My friends and relatives were at a loss as to how they could help. My new friends in Al-Anon (I know now) were waiting for me to finally get worn out enough to give up and let go. My daughter, the "achiever," the "helper," had watched her brother get the lion's share of attention during these crises. She had grown up to be a well-trained enabler and had carved out her own set of life problems. Long ago, she had reached the point of acceptance about my addiction to her brother's potentials and merely rolled her eyes whenever I got caught up in it again.

Somehow, what I felt this time was a little different. The anger, pain, and despair seemed to be gathering into a giant storm cloud and I realized it was time for me to let go of my son or be destroyed myself. That evening, one of the worst and most painful in my life, was also one of the best. I finally came to the end of my long, long rope. I gave up and let go, preparing myself for a drop straight down into a bottomless pit.

But, to my surprise, the fall was quite short and the landing rather gentle. I felt a little glimmer of peace and a tiny beginning of lightness where the thousand-pound load had been for so long. For that moment, I had given up trying to be anyone's savior and desired with all my heart simply to be me … whoever that turned out to be. I had been so absorbed in changing my son's life that my own life had become a mystery to me in many areas. I began to think that what I had heard from the other people in Al-Anon and from my sponsor might just be true. Maybe I could start to experience peace, even if my son continued drinking and using drugs. Perhaps, even if he chose not to have the kind of life I wanted for him, I could still have the kind of life I wanted for myself. But at that moment, it all seemed like a pretty big "perhaps."

Notes

- What thoughts and feelings have you experienced recently?

- In what areas do you feel lost and disconnected from yourself?

Chapter Three

Forgiveness

I sat in a softly lit room at a well-known substance abuse treatment center, surrounded by fifty or so people from all parts of the country. It was a gloriously beautiful autumn day. The trees were a riot of color, there was a nip in the air, and the sky was the bluest of blues. Earlier in the day, as I walked into the main building carrying a suitcase loaded with casual clothes and notebooks to be filled with new ideas, I was flooded with awe and gratitude at the peacefulness of this place. At last a time for myself, a vacation from family crisis and stress. I pledged to myself that during my stay I would not worry about the substitute teacher in my classroom, or what might be happening in my son's life, or how my daughter was getting along while trying to juggle a baby and college classes. This was my chance to find a new path for my life.

"And I will not feel guilty because I'm doing something just for me," I promised myself again.

A wonderful turn of events had brought me here for "professionals-in-residence" training. Even though I was still teaching,

I had become very interested in the field of substance abuse counseling. This was my lucky break. Joan Kroc, the wife of Ray Kroc, the founder of McDonald's restaurant chain, was donating free training for people who worked with children in the San Diego area. Along with my special education background, my work as a liaison between the school district and police department on issues of child abuse and molestation had made me eligible for her generosity. It was also helpful, I must admit, that my soon-to-be-husband was director of her foundation, Operation Cork. He had submitted my name along with others from our area for the gift of training in the field of substance abuse treatment. Not surprisingly, I had chosen to go through the family treatment side of training. No one in the group knew who the "real" family members were and who the fledgling "professionals" were. Only I knew that I was both. I thought it would be my little secret until the chaplain made his opening remarks on the first day.

"Everyone here has something in common," he said.

Darn! One sentence into the very first hour and tears were already stinging my eyes. Of course, I knew what we had in common. We had failed. We had fallen short, and someone we loved was the product of our failures.

"It's not your fault," he continued.

His words sliced through the tangled thoughts of my own guilt and despair. It was the last thing I would have expected him to say.

Some miserable, tired person inside me said to myself, "Please, let it be true."

Maybe I said it to God, but, at that point, I was too angry to speak to Him after all of my unanswered prayers.

The man speaking was a chaplain, a professional therapist, and a substance abuse family specialist, so he must think he was telling the truth. I began to have a small hope that he could show me a path that might lead the way out of this maze of misery I was so lost in.

He said that the only way out of unhealthy situations was to detach, and that true detachment could come only through total forgiveness of others and ourselves, and that total forgiveness could come only from willingness to turn our lives and the lives of those we loved over to a higher power of our own choice. He explained that the only way out was to "let go." In other words, the only person's life anyone can live is their own.

As he spoke, a new idea started to form in my mind that slowly became the essential truth for me. "There is a Higher Power, Barbara, and you're not it."

Of course, that was just the beginning, just the first day, and it took a long time for this new concept to really sink in.

Even in those first moments, the simple reality of his words had started to make sense. I had heard words like that from my parents. Their carefully worded comments usually led to the fact that I could not hold on to my son forever nor could I rescue him from the uncomfortable situations he got himself into. Even though I was careful to leave them in the dark about the extent of his problem, they knew an unhappy situation was unfolding and getting worse. I was equally careful to let the meaning of what they said slide past me unnoticed. I always thought of some friend or acquaintance who would profit from their advice. Interesting what we hear and apply to others but never think that it might apply to us as well.

As I listened to the chaplain on that first day, I began looking forward to the experience. By the time he finished his opening remarks, I had committed myself to giving it my best effort. It would take quite a bit of work on my part, but, if there was a chance I could be free of the dark emotional cave I had been living in, I was willing to work hard for that chance.

But, I wondered, would I be able to make the changes in my own ideas and beliefs about whom and what I was in charge of and let the rest go in order to achieve freedom and serenity? The next question that came to mind was, "Free to be who? Free to do what?"

A large part of my life; all right, to be perfectly honest, the largest part of my life had been wrapped up in working on other people's lives. If I was going to be free to be myself and work on my own life, it felt like going full-sail into uncharted waters.

"Who would I be? What would be my role?" I asked myself.

I told my Al-Anon sponsor later that in the beginning I felt like Swiss cheese from all the holes in myself where I gave up what I considered to be my best "stuff." Who would need me? And I *did* need to be needed. Being needed felt good, no matter how much it hurt, no matter how much I complained.

When the chaplain was talking about forgiveness being a big step toward achieving serenity, I was relieved to hear that forgiveness did not mean that I had to accept unacceptable behavior ever again. Somewhere in my upbringing, I had confused the idea of forgiveness to mean that you should turn yourself into a doormat. This new idea of forgiveness was actually an inside job that would benefit me emotionally, mentally, physically, and spiritually. I liked it.

During the first few days, the new ideas were a little frightening, but staying the way I was seemed more frightening. I was at the bottom with no way to go but up, so I abandoned myself to the family program. That was to have a powerful impact on the rest of my life. What I couldn't be even dimly aware of at that moment was that every positive change in my life would deeply affect everyone around me, even forcing adjustments in relationships that would give other people opportunities for healthy decision-making in their own lives.

Notes

- How have you tried to be in charge of other people's lives?

- Which ways have worked out well?

- Which ways have not worked out well?

- Have you held onto grudges, anger, and unforgiveness?

- How has that harmed you?

Chapter Four

The Beat Goes On ...

After I got home from the treatment center, even though I was practicing the new skills and ideas I had learned and beginning to feel more acquainted with myself and at peace, nothing had changed with my son.

Autumn turned into winter and still his alcoholism and drug dependence marched ahead unabated. He suffered many crises, but I was learning to respond to them less and less. He asked for many things, but my answers became "no" more often than "yes." I was learning the part about detachment. Sometimes I was even able to detach with love.

One portion of the training had included group sessions with family members, professionals, and people who were in treatment all together in one room. None of us knew anyone else in the group or why they were there. One man in his forties shared with us that this was his fifth treatment, but he knew he would stay clean and sober after this one. Anyone could have guessed who the relatives from the family program were. All of us were strained forward in our seats as we listened for the magic ingredient that would make this man stay clean and sober. Maybe we could go home and do it for the addicted person we loved.

He continued, "Now I have to take care of my own sobriety. My mother died, and nobody else will rescue me anymore."

That was a big eye-opener. I imagined my son saying the same thing to a group.

"My mother died, so I'll have to stay clean and sober now. She was the only one who hung on and hung on, willing to do anything to save me."

I wondered, "Should make him wait until I'm dead?" Could I stop rescuing him before he had to wait for my death, or his? It was a good question.

My sponsor had pointedly asked me, "Are you willing to love your son to death just so you won't have to feel the pain of letting him go?"

That one hit home. It hurt because I knew it was true. My motivation for being his savior wasn't a healthy one.

One afternoon, just before the holidays, I found myself talking about some really tough love with my new husband.

"Bob, are you sure we should do this?" I asked.

"Is there anything else left to do?" he responded.

The night before, he had found me pacing around the living room at 3 AM. I told him that I was thinking about canceling all holiday celebrations because I couldn't face the prospect of another special occasion ruined by alcohol and drugs, even though they were not served in our home. The suspense was just too much. Even on those occasions when my son showed up in good shape he was still edgy and defensive. I would feel my whole body tensing up, just waiting to see what was going to happen. It was always the unexpected, and it usually happened when I was just relaxing and starting to tell myself that everything was going to be all right. Slowly, I had started to behave as if I had no control over what happened in my own home. I had volunteered to be a victim by allowing things to continue on the way they had always gone. During that middle-of-the-night talk, we decided to do an intervention on my son before the holidays. We started making careful plans. Canceling the holiday celebrations for the whole family, which now included Bob's family as well as my own, would be letting drugs and alcohol rule our lives, too. So we talked about how to conduct our own little intervention. It had to be planned carefully.

We invited my son over to dinner. We didn't do that very often due to his escalating drinking and drug use, so I was certain he would know something was up. While listening for his car, I went over in my mind what we had decided to say, what tone of voice I was going to use, and what incidents I wanted to talk about. Some of my examples would be hard for my son to hear, and they would be even harder for me to say.

I planned to describe my terror on the night that he had almost pushed me off a balcony in a rage fueled by alcohol and crystal meth. He was furious because I had refused to give him the keys to my car. The next day, when his friends told him what he had done, he showed up at my door, but this time in tears apologizing and telling me how much he loved me. It broke my heart, but from that time on I was afraid of him when he was drinking and using. Once, his sister and I even called the police to take him away from our home, and she and I spent the night in a motel because we were afraid he would come back.

Next, I planned to describe the Easter dinner when he arrived several hours late, obviously high and bringing a lady friend who he belligerently introduced to family and friends as a stripper. Although no one objected to her profession, he continued to behave in such a hostile manner that everyone simply got up and left, including me.

There was the drunken motorcycle accident that he and his pregnant passenger miraculously survived, but required a long hospital stay and a lengthy recuperation at my home. I, of course, volunteered to nurse him back to health only to come home one night to the smell of burning rubber. I discovered that he had gone down to the beach and gotten so drunk that he fell into a fire pit and burned the crutches' rubber handles. I remembered my knees giving way and sitting down hard on the couch. In my ignorance of his addiction, I had thought that the terrible accident had "taught him a lesson."

I decided it would be best not mention too many instances, but I did want to cite examples that carried a lot of emotional pain for me and, hopefully, for him too. I reminded myself to use a steady tone of voice and not add anything more. I had been in too many losing debates with him to think that I could win any sort of argument or discussion. No matter how it started out, I always ended up defending myself and trying to justify anything I had said. I told myself that, no matter what happened, I was going to stay calm, but I still felt myself flinch as I heard his car door close.

The moment he walked in the door, he could tell that something was different. I saw his jaw muscles tighten, but he kept on smiling. We calmly told him that we had been considering canceling all holiday celebrations but had come to the conclusion that we would have to cancel his part in the family instead. We told him that his only gift under the tree would be an envelope that would guarantee substance abuse treatment for him, and he was invited over to pick that up only on the condition that he showed up clean and sober. We added that he had to be in good enough shape so that no one would be nervously waiting for him to explode over some little thing. He would be asked to leave if he appeared to be impaired in any way. I said I hoped he would accept our offer of treatment because I loved him so much and didn't want a repeat of any of the experiences that had been so hard on everyone involved. Then I began a shorthand version of my planned remarks.

At first he sat listening, almost stunned. Then he exploded, bombarding us with four-letter words. He said that if this was the way "family" treated its own, then he didn't need any of us. He told us where we both could go. He raged on for several minutes, saying that his life was going along just fine. He said he was okay and in better emotional shape than any of us.

My husband looked at him steadily and said, "You are not okay. You are pathetic."

I think those words hurt me more than they hurt my son, because they were the very words I had hidden inside my heart for so long. They were the truest words I had ever heard. He stood staring at us as though we were strangers for a moment, and then bolted out the door. I started my old mental litany of responses:

"Maybe we're wrong. Maybe he really isn't using drugs or drinking anymore."

"Maybe, if we just try to make him feel better about himself, he'll pull himself together."

"Maybe we should just try to ignore the situation."

I suppose the endless string of excuses and wishful thoughts could have gone on to infinity but, in my heart, I knew I had taken off my blinders and could never again pretend I didn't see reality. My son was pathetic, and it was time that someone spoke the truth right out loud. Whatever came of it, nothing could be worse than the insanity of going on this way. The lies, the little cover-ups, the "kindness" that looked the other way, the silence, the secrets were all conspiring to keep my son drinking and using until he overdosed or killed himself or someone else in an accident. My Al-Anon sponsor was helping me gradually see that every time I softened a blow or lessened a consequence for my son it took away another opportunity for him to learn and grow through painful consequences of his own faulty decision-making. Looking at it from that point of view, I began to see that all of the people in my son's life who thought they were helping him were literally in the process of loving him to death, the same way I was.

Months later, my son told me the one word that stuck with him and wouldn't let go was "pathetic," because deep inside he knew it was true. Once his anger subsided, he knew that the person who had said it felt he was strong enough to hear the truth with no sugarcoating. And that gave him a strange feeling of pride, but he couldn't understand why. He said that from that time on he began to think about trying to get clean and sober, but it seemed an impossible dream. He had used alcohol and drugs for so long that he could not imagine life without them. But he was scared, too. He was starting to drink and use constantly. In many areas of his life, he was running out of options. Now he was losing his last ties with his family. He started to think that it might be worth a try.

To my great surprise, he did come to our open house on that sunny, California Christmas day. He was gaunt, and his beautiful black hair looked dull and greasy even though it had just been washed. His face looked like a defeated old man. He was nervous and just hung around the open front door for a while before venturing into the living room. He was obviously sober and on his best behavior. One of our recovering friends was telling a hilarious story about how he had gone into treatment about the same time of year and locked himself in the men's room until his wife's threats brought him back into the lobby of the treatment center.

My son took a cautious step in our friend's direction. With a feeling of relief, I saw him smile a little through the tightened muscles around his mouth. But still, he said nothing that day about our offer. When he left, he took the envelope with our note and his only other present, a tin box filled with cookies. Bob's mother had put it there because she couldn't stand to see him leave without a gift. I swallowed a big lump in my throat when he left and said a couple of Al-Anon slogans in my head, probably starting with "Let go and let God." I needed something to drown out the urge to run after him and tell him how much I loved him and try yet again to talk him into getting help. For that moment, I set aside all the anger, rage, hurt feelings, disappointments, and embarrassment. All I had left was love and fear.

I reminded myself for the millionth time, "There is a Higher Power, Barbara, and you're not it."

A few days later, my son dropped by unexpectedly. He seemed distraught. Usually, when he was in that frame of mind, we could count on his visit ending in an unpleasant scene. I felt my stomach twist into its old, familiar knot. However, on this occasion, he was obviously making a real effort to keep himself in check. We talked about what treatment was and what it wasn't. I'd just presumed that he knew what it was all about, but he had some very real fears. At first, he viewed it as a sort of imprisonment where the family could just get rid of him. Then he thought maybe it was a lockup of some sort where other people made him get sober. I explained that, in reality, most substance abuse treatment, especially in a place that stressed the twelve-step approach, was just a time to get the chemicals out of the system in a safe environment, present an education on the disease of addiction, and offer options for a new lifestyle. What he did with that education and those options after he finished his thirty days would be his own business. Bob and I had to go on with our lives, and we wanted to present him with the opportunity to go on with his. Beyond that opportunity, we had nothing more to give him but our love.

After he left, I went over and over the conversation.

"Should I have said more?"

"Should I have said less?"

I was still in the business of tormenting myself because I thought I had so much power in another person's life that I could make it or break it with a conversation. At a meeting that night, I shared my fears and feelings of inadequacy with my Al-Anon sponsor. She looked at me with such patient eyes. She had gone through so many similar experiences with her son. Now I know how many times she must have heard the same stories from different people in different situations, but always with the same dynamics. Yet, at the time, I thought my situation was unique and very special.

On a crisp, sunny day near the end of December, my son called to ask for a ride. He had decided to enter a nearby chemical dependency treatment center. My husband and I got in the car and tried to reassure each other that he would be at the address he had given us, but we were unmasked when we saw him standing outside waiting for us, and both of us let out a breath of relief. He got in the backseat, but he looked like he wanted to jump right back out. I inwardly groaned every time we were stopped by a red light or hindered by a slow driver.

"Get out of the way! Can't you see how important this is?" I wanted to shout each time we were slowed down.

We finally arrived in the parking lot, but I was still frazzled, thinking he might change his mind at the last minute. He gave me a tight little smile and took my hand as we walked through the front door. He was shaking like a leaf. I imagine I was too. The intake person took my son's personal "luggage," a black plastic trash bag containing a few clothes. Everything else consisted of the clothes on his back, an empty wallet, a key that went to nothing, and thirty-six cents. It broke my heart. My handsome, proud, intelligent, beautiful son was reduced to this. At the time, I didn't realize what a miracle it was. He had, indeed, come to the end of his rope, the end of his resources, the end of his relationships, and the end of his ability to cope.

Now he had a chance to get well.

Notes

- What changes would you have to make in order for your life to be more satisfying?

- Who is in charge of making those changes? (**Hint:** If it's anyone other than you, you are already in trouble.)

- How could you make your home a serene, safe place for you to live the way **you** want to live?

Chapter Five

So ... How Long Has Your Son Been Drinking?

The doctor asking this question reminded me of the grandfather I had loved so much. I warmed to the idea of confiding in him whatever he wanted to know.

"I guess since he was about fifteen or early sixteen. That's the first time I saw him drunk. He was a little violent," I said, trying to avoid the humiliating memory of my son and me yelling and pushing each other in the front yard while our small-town neighbors looked on. He was trying to get in the car and drive away, drunk as he was. I remembered ripping the pocket out of a new jacket I had just bought him. I was brought back to the present by the doctor's voice asking another question.

"Marijuana?" the doctor asked.

"Probably in his late teens. I'm not sure he's ever really used marijuana very much," I replied.

"Other drugs?"

"I know he's been using some sort of speed, probably since

his early twenties," I replied. "That's when he really got strange and unpredictable."

As time went by, my son came into the office with us. As he and the doctor talked, I heard him answer the same questions in a much different way.

"Drinking? Oh, I was drinking alcoholically before I turned thirteen," he said. "The first time I drank home brew with my friend, I knew it worked just right for me."

"Pot? Probably a little later the same year. All the drugs I use now I was using to some degree by the time I was fifteen."

I realized that my mouth was hanging open. At lightning speed I was seeing a series of past scenes:

- Our neighbors laughing about what great home brew they made and how it knocked your socks off. Our sons looking at each other knowingly and laughing.

- Taking my son to have his blood sugar tested because it was hard to wake him up in the morning and his mood swings were so wild.

- Sitting in a family counselor's office with my son and daughter, my son's face set in a permanent scowl.

- Yelling at my daughter that she was keeping secrets about her brother. What did she know that I didn't? No answer.

- Sitting in school counselors' offices and hearing the same message time after time. "He's a bright boy, but he doesn't turn in any work. There are all those tardies and truancies. He doesn't seem to care."

What a goon I'd been! How could I have been so blind? So stupid? I didn't understand then how family members lose track of reality while trying to make sense out of senseless behavior, trying to make sanity out of insane situations. I didn't understand what was happening, so I tried to construct answers that would explain the chaos that started when my son was twelve years old and finally led to this day fifteen years later. No wonder I felt crazy from time to time. No wonder I started to doubt my sanity.

Well, I had returned to reality with a thud, but I was starting to understand that my recovery, like my son's, would have to be an ongoing experience. My growth as a person had also been stunted due to my own addiction, the addiction to fixing my son, my addiction to his potentials.

Notes

- Are there any areas of your life that might require a more honest look?

- What have you purposely overlooked because you didn't know what to do about the problem if you faced it?

Chapter Six

Moving in a Positive Direction

When I first began to suspect that I was the only person I could change, I resisted. That's putting it mildly. It slowly occurred to me that many of the changes I had to make were going to be in areas that I considered to be my strongest.

"What's wrong with taking care of the people I love?" I whined to my Al-Anon sponsor. "I can't help it if I'm strong and can handle crises well. Why shouldn't I use that inner strength to help the ones I love? Isn't it my responsibility? After all, they're my children (neighbor, friend, employer, or anyone who *needed* me). Besides, I was raised in a home that taught me to house the homeless, feed the poor, and rescue anyone who needs my help."

I didn't realize how self-righteous my words must have sounded. My sponsor simply referred me to the Bible.

"Read the story of the prodigal son, and try to see what it is teaching," she said. "You'll see that the son took his inheritance and walked to a nearby town. We know it was nearby because later he simply walked back again. The inhabited world was a smaller place. There wasn't a large population then, so there is no doubt that his father knew where he was and what he was doing. But his father did not go after him and drag him home or bribe him to do the right thing. The father simply let go. The father probably heard from relatives or friends in the town about his son's poor behavior, squandering his money and drinking himself into blackouts. After all, when the son finally bottomed out, he was asleep in a pigpen and seemed unsure of how he got there. The son had a moment of clarity when he was in that pigpen and knew what he had to do in order to save his own life. When he walked back home from town, his father saw him from afar and ran to meet him. He knew his son had met the consequences of his actions and was ready to be a member of the family again. The son returned to his family with humility and made amends for his behavior. The father threw a large party and welcomed his son back. Even though he did all of this, the father did not change the other brother's inheritance. What he had would still go to the other brother and it seems clear that the returning son was going to have to make his own way in the world. But the young man was loved and well and in his right mind, so he probably had a good life. That, Barbara, is the example we are given of what a good parent does when their adult child makes poor choices and behaves in an immature and irresponsible way."

I gave her lesson a lot of thought. I had hunted down my son and berated him. I had cajoled, cried, manipulated, made bail, and loaned money. I had blocked or softened every consequence so he would never have to, figuratively, wake up in a pigpen. Had I been helping or harming? I knew the answer to that question. I had not behaved like the good parent in the story of the prodigal son. Not only had my helping and controlling been harmful to my son, but I had also put myself in danger as well, having just had two close brushes with chemical dependency. Once, a physician prescribed tranquilizers because I presented myself with the umpteenth stress-induced ailment. The other time, I discovered that certain diet pills helped me maintain the illusion that I could handle the ills of the world with one nervously trembling hand tied behind my back. Clearly, my picture of myself as a calm, competent parent and helper was developing a few cracks.

As time passed, I learned to be suspicious of the old, warm glow I felt in the very center of my being when someone said:

- "I don't know how you handle this so well. I couldn't take it."
- "You've got to help me with this. I can't turn to anybody else."
- "You're so strong (or caring or patient)."

On several occasions, I needed nothing more than to hear the word "Mom" said in a certain urgent tone of voice over the phone at 3 AM to feel the surge of strength and warmth (coupled, of course, with anger and resentment) that would turn me into Super Enabler Woman, Defender of the Weaker and Less Competent. Off I would fly to help, a curious blend of hero/victim, martyr/saint.

What about the people I flew off to save? What about their opportunities to develop their own strengths? What about their lost chances to grow through hard struggles and tough consequences in order to reach their own best selves? What toll had "going beyond myself" in the name of helping taken on my own life and growth? I might have looked like a saint, but, in truth, I was trampling all over my loved ones' sacred growing grounds and harming myself in the process. It was time to make some changes in a positive direction.

One of the first areas of my "good stuff" that needed looking into was that of being a very good "helper." It feels good to be a helper from time to time. My problem was that I couldn't see the difference between being supportive of someone who was making positive growth in his or her life and being a helper in a caretaking way. I couldn't understand the distinction between being responsible *to* someone and being responsible *for* someone.

When I was busy being a caretaker/helper (and feeling very good about it, I might add), some ideas seemed really important to me:

- I wanted to be sure the people I cared about felt safe and loved *all* the time.
- I felt responsible for ensuring that their experiences left them with high self-esteem and a good self-image (later, I wasn't even sure what those nebulous catch phrases really meant).
- I wanted to be sure they had all of what I considered to be life's necessities.
- I didn't mind sacrificing for them. My needs seemed less important than theirs. I didn't mind making do or doing without so long as I knew their needs and wants were being met. (Picture this one with little rays of light

popping out from behind my head like you see in the pictures of saints.)

- I had to see that they turned out well ... according to *my* standards, of course.

- I wanted them to behave correctly. If they didn't, I saw it as an embarrassment to *me*.

- I had to guide and direct them and be involved in their decision-making. Wasn't I just giving them the benefit of my experience?

- I had to be sure that everyone I loved was in a safe environment. I worried about this a lot, especially in the middle of the night.

- I always did my best to protect them from suffering the consequences of their actions or inactions, never seeing that such "protection" would lead to dire consequences by hampering their growth. It was probably among the most disrespectful things one human being could do to another.

- I was there for them to take over situations they were not strong enough to handle (but I thought I was strong enough to handle "for" them).

- I did my best to act as a buffer between them and their disappointments and failures.

- It was important for me to be a good listener and always be verbally supportive, no matter what.

- I lived by the old family motto, "If we don't look good, what will *they* think?" I still don't know who *they* are, but I sure worried a lot about *them*.

Many of these ideas were a part of my thinking from time before memory. Some had never been examined in the light of day as to whether they were truly helpful or, at some level, quite destructive to the very people I loved most. If you see yourself in any of the above statements and the other person is past infancy, you may have gone from being loving and supportive to being a caretaker. In some circles, you are known as the dread "enabler."

When looked at objectively, many caretaking ideas are belittling and destructive, both to the caretaker and the person receiving the so-called care. These ideas imply the impossible dream, that one person can control and direct another person's actions and feelings. Such ideas imply that certain human beings, those who are being taken care *of*, come into the world and, to a certain extent remain, less able. The cared-for person is not allowed to learn from the good results or the less-than-comfortable natural consequences of acting on their own ideas and choices. They are cheated out of the opportunity to view themselves as independent, competent decision-makers who learn through the outcomes of those decisions.

Too often failure, and the resulting pain, are seen as something bad instead of a natural and necessary step toward success. The truth is that failures lead to small successes that finally lead to mastery. This is a natural progression in all areas of life, including those involving decision-making, growth in maturity, and the slow, but solid, development of true self-esteem. Those steps would have held true for my son as well if I had believed that he could feel pain and grow. Looking back, I am struck with my total lack of faith in the process, in my son, in a Higher Power, in anything but myself and my help.

What was happening to me as I became more and more wrapped up in my helping role? I was becoming more limited and cut off from myself. My identity was getting progressively more tangled up with my son, with who he was and what he was doing rather than who I was becoming and what I was doing. You can see from reading my story that I was clearly a very wounded and unhealthy helper by the time my son was in his mid-twenties.

I also discovered that caretaking was a powerful and effective way to avoid looking at and dealing with my own issues. I felt really lost in many areas of my life and, early in my recovery process, I clung to a few new ideas that seemed startling in their simplicity and common sense. One of the new ideas was that "serenity is minding my own business." I heard that cryptic definition at one of the first open AA meetings I attended years ago. It certainly turned out to be a constant truth for me. In my frenzy of helping, I had forgotten how to mind my own business. In fact, my own business, my own issues, my own mental and physical health, and my own life had gotten into serious trouble while I was trying to fix everyone else.

Remembering a lesson once I had learned it seemed to be a problem for me. It sometimes felt like I made the same mistakes over and over. Finally, I wrote a list of learnings that were important to my own sanity. I have not always adhered to them perfectly, but they have provided me with a framework for reorganizing old, destructive patterns. They are timeless, and I often refer to them when in doubt. They include the following:

- I will not get between another person and the natural

consequences of his/her actions, inactions, or decisions. Natural consequences are the most powerful teachers any of us have.

- I will not bail anyone out of jail or pay his/her fines.
- I will not cover for irresponsible behavior. I will not make excuses, write notes, make phone calls, tell lies, do the job myself, clean up someone else's mess, cover up for their mistakes, and so forth.
- I will not pay fines or debts, cosign notes, or loan money to pay fines, rent, or debts; nor will I do the little charade where I make up some job for the person to do so he/she can pay back the money I would like to loan him/her to get them out of the present jam. (Yeah, I can hear Ms. Nichols, my high school English teacher hissing at me, "Missy, do you know the definition of a run-on sentence?" But that sentence is an example of the way my mind worked in those days, with little run-on convoluted plans to make everything look right even when it wasn't.) I cannot allow myself to pretend the money would be a gift because it's so near a birthday, Christmas, Groundhog Day, or some other silly excuse.
- I will not go along with convenient explanations and excuses for unacceptable or irresponsible behavior. Let's all just stick with reality, please.
- I will not listen to stories that blame others, half-true explanations of the latest problem, or self-aggrandizing tales in which he/she knows more than anyone else and is always right. That legitimizes insanity and wastes more of my precious time.

- I will not change plans in order to respond to the latest crisis.
- My home will not ever again be available as an alternative living arrangement for uninvited "guests," not even for one night.
- I will not do for anyone else what he/she should do for himself/herself. I hear my own arguments about what very sensitive and hurting people they are and how only I truly care enough to help them. But, I won't. Not if I really love them. No matter how hard it is for me to give up my role as helper.
- I have relinquished my role as rescuer. It hurts. It leaves a hole in the middle of me. But I've got to learn to give others the respect of suffering their own pain, learning their own lessons, and enjoying their own growth. I have to care enough to let go and give them the chance to become fully functioning, independent human beings. Obviously, this is going to be a lifetime learning experience, and I'm going to continue to need all the help I can get.

Notes

- Which of the caretaking errors do you recognize in yourself?

- Which ones would you like to change?

- What can be your first step in making that change?

Chapter Seven

The Big "R"—Responsibility

A big problem for me was trying to define the word "responsibility." I never stopped long enough to decide whose responsibility something should be. I just automatically felt responsible for everything. The very thought of that word started a chain reaction something like this:

- **Responsibility:** Something with the word "should" in it.
- **Accountability:** Did I take care of the "should" well enough?
- **Guilt:** No, I didn't. There was a problem, and it must have been my fault.
- **Anger:** No matter how hard I try, why do I always end up feeling guilty?
- **Start over:** I always feel guilty because it was my responsibility and I should have done better.

In our family, this is known as the "toilet bowl syndrome." You just swirl around in circles. Nobody will flush you on down, and you can't pull yourself out. Doesn't sound very healthy, does it?

During the hard times with my son, I was given a new definition of responsibility to think about, compliments of my mother, Dorothy.

She said to me, in total exasperation, "Barbara, don't you know that eventually every tub has to sit on its own bottom?"

I wasn't sure my relationship dynamics could be changed so that every tub would be able to sit on its own bottom, so I privately went to my Al-Anon sponsor and other people I hoped would give wise counsel on the subject. They suggested the following behaviors:

- **Let go of regretting, feeling guilty, or being angry about the past. The past is *past*. It can't be changed.** No more rehashing the past by rewinding and fast-forwarding old tapes to see where the situation went wrong or what could have been done to make it turn out differently. My words and actions were not so important or powerful or necessary as imagined. Worst of all, I had been wasting time from my own life by regretting and fretting over things that could not be changed. If I had known better, I would have done better. From the beginning of time, people could only do their best with who they were at the time.

- **Give up all statements starting with "if only."** Oh, man! Did that ever eliminate a lot of the constant chatter in my head.

- **Get on up out of the pity pot.** Now, this was a really life-changing new behavior. When I gave up being a victim, I had to give up all the people and things I had blamed for every unhappy circumstance in my life. I had to give up my power to control others through guilt. I finally had to take total responsibility for what I did, how I felt, how I behaved, and the decisions I made. I had to admit that I was totally responsible for me and others were totally responsible for themselves, their own decisions, and their own lives.

- **No blaming.** Blaming turned out to be a big waste of my time and accomplished nothing for anyone involved. A big bonus was when I realized I didn't need to place blame on myself either. I could just admit when I was wrong, make amends if needed, spend a few moments thinking how to do it better next time, and then let it go.

- **No more asking "why?"** I started to understand at a deep level that asking "why?" was the biggest time waster of all. Our brain is built to go after that question like a heat-seeking missile, and it can find a million targets. But all those answers never really help the situation and usually just lead to more blame. It wastes time that could be used more constructively.

- **Stop acting like a martyr.** Being a martyr also turned out to be a big waste of time. Being a martyr felt good in an awful sort of way. It had gotten me a lot of attention and it had given me the power to control others by making them feel guilty, but it was terribly destructive to me and those around me. No matter how much of a saint I looked like or how much I liked starring in the "ain't it awful" drama, I was again just wasting time and retarding my own growth. My sponsor kept reminding me, "There are no victims, only volunteers."

- **No more telling people off, being harsh, or having tantrums.** Darn! That stuff felt good at the moment, but it only turned out to be addictive and destructive in an awful way. I had to find other ways to let off steam and deal with stress a little at a time. Being trapped in the caring, sweet, good person role that I had built for myself meant that I had to hold everything in until I reached the boiling point. Then look out! My outbursts were as shocking to me as they were to everyone else when I finally "blew." It sure got everyone's attention, but not for very long, and never accomplished anything positive for me or anyone else in the long run.

- **Let go of being critical and judgmental of others.** This has been an ongoing struggle. I have to admit that even now my rapier wit and I are sometimes reduced to silence.

- **Get real, and give up living in fantasy.** This meant that I had to give up my slightly edited versions of "the way it used to be" as well as wishful thinking about "how it will be when …" I had to start by taking small steps toward total honesty and living each day, each hour, in reality. It took a lot of guts. I had lived for so long in a hopeful fantasyland where everything and everyone had the happy ending I wanted for them. Looking at stark reality was a tough situation, which included the fact that everything might not have a happy ending and not everyone wanted for themselves what I wanted for them. Giving up my fantasies, butting out of other people's business, and leaving things between them and their own Higher Power turned out to be a one-day-at-a-time job.

- **Without placing blame or feeling hurt or angry, become aware of what is *really* happening and honestly start looking at your own part.** My part was the only part that was my responsibility.

- **Realize that none of us are in charge of any outcomes.** That's the Higher Power's job, and knowledge of that fact continues to give me permission to take a break.

- **Learn to use the magical question when others present you with a problem or crisis that is not of your own making: "What are *you* going to do about that?"** That question has done more to change my life and the lives of those around me for the better than any other single strategy. There is no other question in the human language that implies so much respect and confidence in the other person. It is a question that truly fosters the ability for every tub to sit on its own bottom.

Another strategy that has been useful in restoring objectivity in the face of upsetting situations is to imagine myself sitting in the balcony of a theater watching a play. I imagine that the play turns out to be my life as it is right now. Staying calm and objective in my balcony seat, I watch the action and listen to the dialogue.

I ask, "What is my character's role? What is really happening? What is my part in the action?"

From my balcony seat, I decide whether I am watching a comedy or a tragedy. Often, it turns out to be a little of both. And, from further down the road, some situations that seemed to be the most tragic at the time now seem the most comical.

Sometimes, when watching a play or a show on television, we would like to yell advice to the characters:

- "Don't go in there!"
- "Don't lie! Tell the truth, you ninny!"
- "Oh, no! Nobody's dumb enough to fall for that one!"

Right now, say out loud what you would like to say to the character that is you in the play. Whatever you just said was probably pretty good advice.

Notes

- Make a list of what you see as your responsibilities.

    Go back and cross out the ones that could, and should, be taken care of by the person whose responsibility it **really** is. (Try to think of your loved one as the next-door neighbor rather than a relative or someone you love. If you were taking care of this responsibility for the next-door neighbor, would it be a healthy thing for either of you?) Write "them" beside the items that belong to someone else.

    Cross out the ones that are final outcomes or final solutions, such as "make them behave the way I want them to behave" or "stop their drinking and/or drugging" or "make them become good and loving sons, daughters, or parents." Those are too big for you and too big for the other person. They are processes, not events. They are too big for a human being, so they must be a responsibility that belongs to a Higher Power. Put "HP" beside those items.

- The unmarked items are probably your responsibility. Most will be about you, not anybody else.

- You can put healthy energy into those responsibilities without creating more problems.

Chapter Eight

The Fatal "F"—Fear

"Fixers," "rescuers," "enablers," whatever you want to call people who find themselves being chronic caretakers and helpers, are people who often get stuck in their roles. Ironically, these people share some overpowering fears, some of which are:

- Their own death or the death of the ones they love.
- Their own emotional pain and the pain of watching those they love suffer.
- Abandonment if they don't meet the needs, demands, or expectations of others.
- Criticism, judgment, being found at fault, or not living up to some ideal image.
- Reality, which often causes them to take refuge in fantasy until reality beats them over the head.
- Codependents fear their own dependency.
- Controllers fear being controlled, being out of control, or losing control of those they feel responsible for. Controllers often lash out at the ones they love when closeness makes them feel vulnerable.

- In general, many helpers are so afraid of pain, abandonment, and death that life cannot be fully lived nor joy fully embraced.

How on earth do people get rid of this kind of fear? Oddly enough, the first step is to acknowledge the fact that fear can never be totally eliminated. The simple acceptance that fear is a normal part of life helps to create a comfort zone with reality. For me, the next step was to acknowledge my fears. The realization that fear was, and will always be, a natural part of reality led to my acknowledgment that trying to wish fear away rather than facing it was hampering my own growth. I decided to make a list of my fears by using simple statements.

I immediately saw that many of my fears were for others and decided the healthiest thing would be to share my concerns with the people I was fearful for. The trick was to share my concern without using it as an opportunity to employ my old friends, manipulation and guilt. I would have to simply state my fears as objectively and calmly as possible.

One of my worst fears concerned the potential suicide of my son. I knew I had to address that issue in a calm, supportive way. Even though suicide threats are often used as manipulative tools (especially by those addicted to chemical substances) to keep others hooked into the problem, such threats should not be minimized or ignored. My son had implied on several occasions, and stated on one occasion, that he wanted to die. All those occasions occurred during situations when I was not responding the way he wanted, but they were frightening all the same, and left me in a state of chronic worry. A suicide prevention specialist told me that openly acknowledging suicide potentials could actually diffuse them. I began to feel that it would be okay to talk about this subject with him, and I did one evening over dinner in a "neutral-zone" restaurant. I simply told him that I loved him and feared he might either take his own life or lose it in an accident or overdose situation. I also told him that the sort of depression that leads to suicide is often a physiological or emotional result of alcohol or drug use, including prescription drugs, and passes in a short while if not acted on. I gave him a suicide prevention hotline phone number. I said I really felt powerless in this area and hoped he would contact a professional if he felt he needed help, but I was not a suicide prevention specialist and feared I would just make matters worse.

The incident that led to this conversation concerned a call I got from my son saying his car had been impounded and he needed money in order to reclaim it. At this point, I had come to the realization that every "yes" answer I gave him prolonged his use of alcohol and drugs and perhaps even freed up the money that might buy that very overdose I was so worried about.

So, after listening to his latest crisis and need for money, I uttered the one word that was so very hard for me to say: "No."

He said, "Then I don't know what else to do except to just walk out into traffic." And with that, he hung up on me.

I was frantic. I knew he was calling from a waiter job he had held briefly. I paced the floor wondering what on earth to do. The only thing I could think of was to call my daughter and tell her about my fear. She was in nursing school and had a crisis phone number list.

She said, "Just stay calm, Mom. I'll call to give him a number where he can get help."

She called back a few minutes later, laughing. "Here's my conversation with that guy you're crying about. I called him and said, 'Buddy, Mom is scared you are going to kill yourself and I'm calling to give you a suicide hotline number.' And he replied, 'F— off! I've got customers waiting for their food here.'"

Almost sucked back into the vortex of the storm again. But still, it left me feeling shaken and helpless, in spite of the fact that I had accidentally done the most helpful thing.

After that situation, I wanted to learn everything I could about suicide, so I talked to several suicide prevention people. Here's what I was told:

- Recognize the main thing you can do is offer information, stay calm, be supportive of the person getting help and, in a crisis immediately call an intervention agency, such as the police. You can explain that thoughts of suicide are often drug induced and will pass when the drug is out of the system. You can encourage the person to wait, seek help, and stay calm while help is on the way. What you cannot do is control the outcome of someone else's decision. Suppose you chose to give up living your own life and became a captive to their threats, even going to the extent of being tied to their side? You would eventually have to sleep and then the responsibility of living or dying would ultimately still be theirs.

- Even though it is hard to accept, you must admit the following facts: If someone is intent on dying, only he or she can save himself or herself by being open to help. You are not God. You can only express love and concern and then present options. The final decision will never be yours. It will be never be your responsibility, regardless of how much you would like it to be.

I know of very few family members of chemically dependent people who have not, at one time or another, been emotionally or financially blackmailed by these sorts of threats. I had no idea how to handle it when my turn came. Because my daughter was in nursing school and had access to crisis hotline numbers, I accidentally did the wisest thing, if only through desperation. Fortunately, my son's decision was to live. Had it been otherwise, I can easily see from this distance that there would have been nothing I could do to stop it. In fact, staying tied into the sick dynamic would only have given him further opportunity to get to a deeper depression. It might have even worsened his chances of making a life-affirming decision.

Notes

- Make a list of your fears.

- What actions could you take that would give you some relief from them?

Chapter Nine

The Big "D"—Detachment
Here's the Catch: *Detachment With Love*

One of the first things I learned about addiction was that there is only one healthy way out of the addictive process. No matter what you are addicted to, the only way out is to let go of the addictive substance. What a shock when I realized that I was so addicted to my son's potentials and to "fixing" him in order for him to reach those potentials that I had actually let my own personal life and health hit an all-time low. For a helper/enabler such as me, I had to let go of the person I was addicted to helping/fixing/enabling.

This step was awfully hard for me. My first attempts at detaching will probably seem quite primitive to you. I unplugged my phone at night. I hid in the linen closet when I saw my son coming up the sidewalk. But, primitive or not, those first steps kept me from minding my son's business for a while. I had a little rest from responding to the next crisis because I didn't know what the crisis was. When he tried to contact me through friends or relatives, I asked them not to deliver his messages and refused to listen if they would not honor my request.

I lost one of my dearest friends during this period. Her daughter was also addicted to alcohol and drugs. My friend and I had been supporting each other in our enabling activities and most of our conversations were built around the "ain't it awful" theme. When I started making some healthy changes in my behavior, she saw it as abandoning my child (never mind that the "child" was twenty-six years old). She told me I was an awful mother, and she suddenly found that we had nothing in common. She invited my son to stay at her place, which happened to be next door to my place, because she "understood" him. Of course, in a few weeks, she was calling to complain of his irresponsibility and immaturity, as though I had asked her to take him into her home. I had to tell her, in all honesty, that her decision to invite him in was not my problem. She hung up on me.

I missed her friendship, but soon found that I was starting to attract a new kind of friend. In the Al-Anon group I was attending, everyone seemed to talk a lot about reality, about honest feelings, and about living each day to the fullest. I started to feel a little hopeful about myself and life in general. I learned some things that helped me get on with the detaching with love process and I'll share them with you:

- Admit that you may be as addicted to another person's potentials as any addict is to his or her drug of choice. Don't be surprised if you see this element cropping up in other relationships as well.

- Recognize that you do not see reality when you are obsessed with fixing another person. When asked to describe the person, often you will not describe the reality of his or her present situation or behavior. You will respond with what they were in the past or who they could be "if only," but not the reality of *now*.

- Realize that you may call it "love," but it's probably mixed with a heavy dose of obsession and, if truth be known, a little dose of anger that verges on hatred.

- Accept that letting go, or detaching, from your obsession with the other person is the course of action that will produce the most health and benefits for you both. Realize that letting go is a process, not a willpower issue or one big event.

- If you find yourself getting into or even creating another crisis, stop! Being part of a constant crisis gives the temporary feeling of being a star in the drama. It gets us a lot of attention and keeps the old adrenaline pumping. Life can seem pretty darn dull without any crisis, but give yourself a period of adjustment. After a while, you'll start to feel more comfortable with a healthy, happy lifestyle.

- Observe your physical and emotional responses when you fall back into your old behavior of trying to control other people and things. Accept the fact that there is a healthier way to live. Besides, how many times have you really been able to control anybody or anything? That's ulcer-making stuff.

- Go ahead and just abandon yourself to the idea of total forgiveness for everyone in your life and every situation. In other words, open yourself to the idea of detaching from the other person's problems and potentials. It may go against the grain to give up old resentments, as well as old hopes, but it will save your emotional fanny. Consider attending a twelve-step group such as Al-Anon, getting a sponsor, and working the twelve steps.

• Start the process of forgiving yourself for your own imperfections and humanness. Give yourself credit for the good things you have done and the efforts you have made. I've cut myself some slack by saying, when beset with guilt, "Honestly, if I'd known better, I'd have done better. I did the best I could do with who I was at the time." And so did my parents, and their parents, and on and on. We are all fallible human beings who do the best we can. That's all we can do. We need to be reminded of that fact often.

• Since serenity is truly minding your own business, write down three ways you can start minding yours. How can you start cutting the cords to those you presently have in a loving stranglehold and start getting a life of your own? In the process, you will give them the priceless gift of having to get a life of their own, too. What issues have you left unattended in your own life that you can start addressing right now? I followed a suggestion from my sponsor that proved to be very helpful, even though it may sound a little too simple. I cut a picture of eyes out of a magazine and taped them on the bathroom mirror. When I saw those eyes looking at me every morning, it reminded me that the person I was responsible for and needed to be working on that day was *myself*. And I needed to do it lovingly.

- Let yourself see, as time goes by, how things can start to get straightened out without your help or interference.

- Try to keep firmly in mind that you no longer have to be a part of the drama or comedy. Nor do you have to come up with solutions for any of the problems you see, including the problem of seeing others become the big "fixer" you used to be. You can't control them either, so just let go of the whole situation.

- Notice how you grow stronger, healthier, and less willing to be manipulated with each time you successfully let go.

- Any problems sent out as hooks to pull you back into the action can easily be deflected by the magical question, "What are *you* going to do about that?"

- Finally, when all the helpers are worn out and used up, you may see the immature/irresponsible person take on his/her own problems and start to grow.

- Be patient. Keep reminding yourself that this is a process, not an event. It will take time. Don't think it is the happy ending when someone decides to get clean and sober or get help in some other way. That is just the beginning. Sobriety from alcohol and drugs is the prerequisite for recovery, but recovery itself is a lifelong, ongoing process. And it's wonderful. And it's painful. And it's real.

Once again, take a balcony seat to observe the drama/comedy of your life taking place on the distant stage. See the ways you have tried to control the other characters and arrange the action. Now, in all honesty, how successful have you been? Have you really succeeded at making things turn out the way you wanted? Have the characters followed your directions? Have you seen long-lasting growth in their maturity and sense of responsibility due to your efforts? Are you ready to admit defeat? If so, find something white. Wave it in the air over your head. Repeat after me: "I give up."

Congratulations. You have just started a new life.

Notes

- What is your only way out of the present mess? (*Hint:* Reread the first two sentences of this chapter.)

- List some ways that you can start letting go right now.

Chapter Ten

Meanwhile, in Treatment

Earlier in this story, I told you about my son entering treatment on that golden, sunny day full of blue skies. I mentioned that I was a twisted wreck by the time we got to the address he had given us, worried he might change his mind and not be there. On the way to the treatment center, my heart nearly lurched out of my chest with every slow car in front of us and every red light. I wanted to scream at everyone to get out of our way. Couldn't they see that we needed a straight, clear road between the treatment center and us? Slow, plodding, insensitive drivers! Well, we finally got there and went through the admission. My son had thirty-six cents in his pocket, his clothes in a trash bag, and a key that went to nothing, and that's how we left him. We were told not to come back for two weeks and that we would not be hearing from him during that time. When we got home, I felt my whole body starting to relax, and I realized I was about to spend the first night in years with no worries about my son. I knew he was safe for the night, and I felt a little sliver of hope. My husband, on the other hand, was still worried that things might not go just right. It was a weekend admission, after all. What if they were short-staffed on Sunday? He decided he had better call the center and give them some insight into my son's problems. They were very cordial and invited us over the next morning. The counselor on duty gave us a warm smile when we walked in and started talking before my husband could say a word.

He said to my husband, "This man is an adult. I see on the forms that your wife attends a family twelve-step meeting. I know you are a substance abuse counselor yourself and attend AA. Now I suggest that you go to Al-Anon too. But I suggest that you and your wife attend separate meetings, at least in the beginning, so you can be totally honest in your sharing without worrying about what each other might think. In fact, here's a meeting schedule. You can go to one tonight."

I was feeling like the "good girl," going to my own twelve-step meetings and all, until he turned his kind face toward me and quietly asked, "And what are you going to do with all that anger you have bottled up?"

"Me, angry?" I sputtered, visualizing a big lump on his forehead just in the spot where I'd like to hit him. "I'm just happy and relieved, not angry," I said with as kindly a look on my face as I could muster.

He told me I would have an opportunity to address family issues during the family week at the treatment center, but in the meantime, I might want to spend some time working on my own issues. I realized I had a few problems of my own, but I still labored under the illusion that once my son was straightened out, most of those problems would resolve themselves.

Then he asked the million-dollar question, "Are you working the Al-Anon steps with a sponsor?"

"Sure," I lied. but without much gusto.

Until that point, I had mainly thought about what Al-Anon could give me, not what I needed to do in order to work the program. My sponsor had been saying more or less the same thing. "If you're not working the steps, don't tell people you're in Al-Anon. Just tell them you're a visitor," she said one evening.

I called the next day and made an appointment to start working the steps with her. From that time on, I got really serious because I knew what the counselor said about my anger was true, even though I didn't totally understand why.

I eventually had two sponsors. Even though I kept my personal sponsor, my husband and I found a wonderful couple who agreed to sponsor us together. Thank goodness we found them at that point because we were about to confront as big a problem as we had faced yet. As my son's thirty days in treatment were nearing an end we got a call from him asking if he could come home for "a few days" when he got out, just until he found a place to live. That doesn't sound too unreasonable, does it? But we knew from our sponsors that the answer to that question could be deadly. They had said yes to such a request and their son had relapsed on his third day home. They explained it to us. When he came home to an environment where he was the son instead of his own man, where all sorts of feelings (like my submerged anger) were swirling around unspoken, where he was likely to see old friends (make that old friendly users and dealers), where he would not be in an environment with other recovering people, he would be a sitting duck for relapse. So, we had their encouragement to love our son enough to say "No."

He was flabbergasted. He repeated the request slowly, as though we hadn't understood him the first time. We gave him as logical an explanation as we could. His response was that he had tried to get into several halfway houses and been turned down by all of them.

We gave him the answer that was to serve us so well as time went by: "That sounds really unfair, but what are you going to do about that?"

With desperation in his voice, he said, "The only person I know who would let me stay with him is my old drug dealer."

That statement had the predictable chilling effect, but we had made a commitment to stand our ground, regardless of what was thrown at us. So we made the statement we had agreed on.

"You know that will be risky. But it's your decision, not ours. Our love and our prayers are with you."

After a long pause, he said, "Guess I could try calling another halfway house, but I don't have much hope of getting in one."

You can imagine how we tied ourselves in knots over that conversation. We went to a meeting that night and everyone was so supportive. But I still found myself up greeting my old friend, Mr. Three AM, looking out my usual middle-of-the-night window, saying a prayer for my son. On the last day of his stay in the treatment center, the last halfway house on the list accepted him. He called to tell us, proud as anything. He had done it himself.

We visited him infrequently during the year he lived in the halfway house. The management discouraged frequent visits or gifts, particularly cash, and with good reason. Hard work needed to be done there. Growing up and gaining maturity was not an easy job. After a specified entry time, we were able to visit with him and take him to lunch. We were waiting downstairs for him when I heard the gruff voice of the house supervisor, a retired Navy chief.

"I'm not your mama, and I don't clean up your mess or cover for you when you're late. You missed kitchen duty this morning, and you will now have it for another week. And you will be on time. Make that bed so it looks decent before you leave this room. It's grow-up time, son."

I was thinking how satisfying it would have been to say exactly that to my son on many occasions when, who came down the stairs looking sheepish and saying he had to do his kitchen duty before he could visit with us? My son. And, as time passed, he grew to love that man who had been berating him, coming back to see him for guidance and friendship for years afterward.

We didn't know too much about my son's daily life. We knew he worked part-time, went to in-house AA meetings every day, and often went to meetings at the treatment center. My husband occasionally attended house meetings when they were open to outsiders. Also a recovering alcoholic, he still attends AA meetings after decades of sobriety. He loves the program and wants to give back to newcomers what he was given when he first came. We took my son to lunch every few weekends and caught up with each others' news. He seemed more mature with each visit, and we were happy for him.

Shortly before the year was over at the halfway house, we had been invited to a meeting to see "our" (we truly felt like a family by then) son receive his one-year coin. He asked my husband to give it to him. Before cake was served, I was asked to say a few words.

Basically, I said, "I am a very grateful mother today. I am grateful for my son's addictions, and I'm grateful for his recovery. If he hadn't had addictions, I wouldn't have had the opportunity to grow in my own recovery program. We would not be a twelve-step family. We would not all be speaking the language of recovery and gratitude on a daily basis. I would still not have a framework for problem-solving that lets me look at my part and change it for the better. In a strange way, I'd have to say that his addictions have been one of the best things to happen to me in this life."

Then we hugged, said the Serenity Prayer, and started to serve the cake.

A young man came up to me and asked if I really meant what I'd said. I replied that I'd never meant anything more.

He said, "I wish my parents felt that way. I can't talk to them about anything. We just pretend that none of this ever happened."

I thought, "Without my own twelve-step program, I think I would have handled things the same way his family did."

That was how my family had handled my uncle's alcoholism and addiction. One of my aunts would lean over close to my mother's ear and say, "Pee Wee is 'you know' again."

The whole family knew what that meant. It meant he was drinking again and pretty soon someone would have to bail him out of jail. When it was our turn to bail him out, I would ask my mother why we were going to the jail to get him again.

She would reply, "Because he's family." Nonsense statements that spoke volumes. They were the only two phrases that were needed where that uncle and several others were concerned. In fact, I had used those two phrases about my own son until I learned more about the disease of addiction and was able to speak words that better expressed reality.

Do you have any phrases like that in your family? Are there any secrets? Do you wish you could speak freely, openly, honestly, and lovingly? Well, you can. You can make the choice to live an open, honest, and peaceful life.

My son's year in the halfway house came to an end. He had been working at a part-time job and had saved up some money, but not enough for a place of his own. What do you think happened then? If you thought we got another phone call about him coming home, you were right.

And, what do you think we said? We said, "Honey, we are so proud of you. You've managed so well and made all your own decisions. You can't come home, but we have every confidence in your ability to take care of your own affairs. What are you going to do about this?"

What he did, at the last minute, was move in with some recovering guys. But after a while, he moved in with a girl who had four adorable kids, and a habit of going bowling with the girls on Thursday night and drinking herself under the score-keeper's table before snorting a little cocaine. Oh, my! Not what we had in mind. Remembering that serenity was minding our own business, we kept out of his business, said a lot of prayers, and spent a lot of time with our sponsors. That relationship and that phase of his life passed. We saw that he was attempting to act responsibly and maturely when the inevitable breakup came. He mentioned when visiting us that he was continuing to work his program by seeing his sponsor and often went back to the halfway house to attend meetings and visit with his friends there. We firmly kept in mind that it was his life, his decisions, and not our responsibility, no matter what the outcome. Eventually, he made it through that experience without a relapse and slowly started to get on his feet in his own life.

One real breakthrough was when we went out to dinner with him and he insisted on picking up the check. At last, we were all adults having dinner instead of parents buying dinner for the "kid." It's true what the old song says. "Little things mean a lot."

We've watched his recovery with wonder and awe. Sometimes it has been like watching a narrowly averted plane crash. Sometimes it has been a thing of beauty. It has been life.

Whenever he works the steps again, I know it because I get a call saying something like, "Mom, I must have been hell to raise. I want to tell you I'm sorry and thanks for all your love."

Once he called and just said, "Mom, thanks for letting me live to get grown. You must have wanted to throw me over the bridge more than once."

All the things I had held inside, all of that anger over the awful times we went though, has slowly melted away. I see my son as a wonderful man coming from behind in maturity and struggling with issues most men overcame at a younger age, but all the same, continuing with solid growth in all areas. I am very proud of him.

I look back on the first time we were allowed to visit him

after he entered the substance abuse treatment program and my absurd hope that I would find a fully healed person who had miraculously gained years in maturity and responsibility in two weeks. What I saw was my own son, finally, looking out at me from behind those beautiful, clear eyes. And suddenly, that was enough. I had my "boy" back, and he was on his way to becoming a man. All I had to do was keep my hands off his life, mind my own business, realize that it takes time to rebuild trust, and let go and let God.

Notes

- What are you most angry about?

- Who are you most angry with? Don't leave out the anger you may feel toward yourself.

- List three actions you might take in order to start recovering from your anger.

Chapter Eleven

Life After Treatment

There is much wisdom in the saying, "Sobriety is the prerequisite for recovery." In other words, recovery is impossible without sobriety from all mood-altering drugs, and that always includes alcohol, no matter what the perceived drug of choice has been. For decades, people have attained sobriety and recovery through twelve-step and other programs. For the lucky few who are afforded formal treatment and have time to dedicate themselves to a concentrated recovery, that recovery and the avoidance of relapse can be greatly enhanced by some form of sober-support living. Solid and long-lasting recovery often results from aftercare facilities and halfway-house living after treatment. The social worker at any treatment facility will be in touch with sober-support living, ranging from exclusive high-dollar places to equally wonderful places for people who have no money at all. Usually, "free" sober-support living will include some sort of self-support through outside work, which in itself can be a very therapeutic adjunct to recovery. The point is, there is something available for everybody.

For those who do not have the opportunity for treatment and do not have a social worker to guide them through the process, the following organizations are only the tip of the iceberg for where a person can find information about substance abuse treatment, support for sobriety, and long-term sober living:

- Council on Alcoholism
- Local substance abuse treatment centers
- Local Mental Health Association
- Salvation Army
- Volunteers of America
- Alcoholics Anonymous
- Narcotics Anonymous
- Your state's agency on alcoholism and drug addiction
- Oxford Houses, if available in your area

Lots of choices, and none of them are yours. If you must do something, the best idea is to do a little research and get as many phone numbers as you can. Make a list. Hand the list to the person who needs treatment and/or long-term sober living. Let them do their own legwork from there. A better result is guaranteed. There will be nobody to blame, nobody to complain to, and a lot of growth in the process.

Notes

- List the results of your research.

Chapter Twelve

In Closing

At the time I started this recovery journey, my life felt like such a mess. I didn't see any place to start making things better. I went to my first Al-Anon meeting in a very confused state. God seemed to have totally abandoned me. None of what I prayed for and wanted so much for the people I loved had worked out (not *my* way, anyway), and I was awash in anger, frustration, and hurt. If you have some of those feelings, I hope this little book has been of some help. As they say, take what you want, and leave the rest.

If you are like me and always want to know the rest of the story, I'll tell you the rest of mine so far. I still trust my twelve-step friends to help me stay in reality. I still tend to think I know best and need constant reminders from my sponsor, who is my dearest and closest confidant and friend, that everyone I love has the same right to mess up and learn from it as I do. I try not to enable anyone. My saving and fixing has caused too many near catastrophes in my life and the lives of those I love. I try to practice living just one day at a time, but that is an occasional toughie, too.

The son I talked about is now in his twentieth year of recovery, and I have gratefully observed many miracles in his life. We are so fortunate to live in the same town with him and his wife, and I am flooded with joy and gratitude every time I see his smiling face. My husband and I have a marriage that we try to live one day at a time, using the twelve steps. That has helped us over the inevitable bumps life gives us. I will always think of my Al-Anon meetings as the most potent form of ongoing self-help and personal growth to be found anywhere. And the price is certainly right.

The next generation is coming along in our ever-expanding family. They range in age from a few months to early twenties. We watch as they struggle through the landmines set in their path by present-day life. Because we know the age of first purposeful use is now below eleven years of age in the United States and that the citizens of our country use a disproportionate amount of all drugs produced on the planet, we have done what we can to inform and educate these precious ones about our family disease. At the very least, they have a higher-than-average chance of being genetically predisposed to addiction, and they need to know it. But we're not so naive as to think we can override hundreds of hours of glamorous "fun" alcohol and chemical use portrayed by the media. Nor do we think grandparents can exert more influence than peers. We can only offer them the benefit of our knowledge and the assurance of our love, and then watch as these little "tubs" we love so much grow up and sit on their own bottoms in a very perilous world.

And, last of all, if anything you have read seems to relate to your life and if you wish things were different, I will leave you with a gift in the form of a magical question:

What are you going to do about that?

Notes

- What ideas come to you when you ask yourself, "What are you going to do about that?"

Additional Materials

Loss of Control Starts the Downward Spiral for Alcohol/Drug User AND Family

Steps to Addiction

Loss of Control

Addiction Increases

At onset of addiction emotional growth stops, maturity stops, spiritual growth stops. Person operates at that level until recovery begins.

Tolerance Builds. More of the substance required for the same effect.

Abuse - Many teen deaths due to driving under the influence.

"Partying"

User's addiction to drug(s) of choice takes charge of his/her life.

LIES, BLAMES, MANIPULATES

SOCIAL: Joins the "Liar's Club." Lies constantly. Others Lie for him/her.

LEGAL PROBLEMS: Jail, divorce court, Bankruptcy Court Drug Court, etc.

FINANCIAL: Financial problems. Financially drain others around them.

JOB: People at work notice substance-related impairment. Series of short-term jobs.

HEALTH: User is in danger of accidents, violence, overdose.

INSANITY OR DEATH

Family's addiction to user's potential results in need to fix or save.

FAMILY: 7 to 10 family, friends, coworkers affected.

SOCIAL: Joins the "Ain't It Awful" club and complains to others. Joins the "Drama Club" and stars in the ongoing crisis.

LEGAL: Pays fines, makes bail, hires lawyers, Loans money for rent, cars, carries the financial responsibilities during "troubled" times.

FINANCIAL: Family has substantial outlays. Think they are "victims" but are really "volunteers."

JOB: Becomes a poor employee with mind always on the substance abuser.

HEALTH: Often the codependent's health suffers first. Stress-related illness, absent-minded accidents, victimization.

INSANITY OR DEATH

Addiction progression chart

Explanation of the
Addiction Progression Chart

This is an explanation of the progression of addiction drawing on the previous page. The arrows going up the left side of that page is the onset of use, abuse, and then addiction. When the addiction reaches "Loss of Control," you see that the chain of events diverges and starts downward. The downward journey on the left is the person with the addiction. The chain going down on the right side is the family and others closely involved. Ironically, both progress downward through exactly the same steps and can ultimately suffer the same consequences at the bottom of the journey.

Please use this guide to study the chart. It is an important part of your education. On the chart, locate the following steps of addiction:

Use	All drinking/drug use starts innocently, usually in a family, social, or fun setting. The age of first use in America is now below eleven years of age.
Addictive Process	The user develops tolerance for the drug(s) of choice, thus requiring more of the substance to produce the same results.
Emotional, Maturational, and Spiritual Growth Stops at the Onset of Addiction	Family members often comment on a loved one's immaturity or irresponsible/self-centered behavior; for example, a thirty-two-year-old who behaves more like a teenager. During recovery, this growth may be regained by working the twelve steps or participating in a recovery group of their choice, and having counseling if needed. It's very helpful for the family to also be involved in their own recovery program.
Loss of Control	This term describes any addiction. Many people can control how long they go without drinking or using, but, in the case of addiction, they cannot predict when they will stop or how much they will use once they have picked up the next drink or drug.

Progression **User's Addiction to Drug(s) of Choice.** **Family's Addiction to User's Potential.**	Progression can be observed on both sides of the chart, the addicted person as well as the family or significant other side. All start the slide downward through "family, social, legal, financial, job, health, insanity, or death." By locating where you see yourself on the chart at this time, you might predict your next problem area as well as whether you are moving in an upward or downward direction.
Symptoms and Family Issues	This is not a moral issue. It is a health issue. Like all health issues, it has symptoms. The first symptom of addiction is lying. The second symptom is blaming. The family is progressively affected. They know they are being told lies, but they do not know about what or why. They start to develop their own addiction, that is, the addiction to fixing the addicted person so he or she can meet his or her potentials. The family becomes addicted to the addict's potentials. They devote a great deal of time, attention, and resources to their efforts to fix or help, often neglecting others and even themselves in the process.

Social Clubs	This is one way to describe the actions of everyone involved. The addicted person begins to associate with others with similar interests, including alcohol and drugs. They become fellow members of the "Liar's Club." The family moves toward people with similar interests or problems and forms the "Ain't It Awful Club," consisting of phone calls and conversations, repeatedly going over the awful situation. The "Drama Club" permits family, friends, and the addicted person to star in the constant crisis around them. Life becomes a series of dramatic scenes.
Legal	Legal problems affect the drinker/user and all those close to him or her. These problems could end in divorce court, bankruptcy court, jail for assault, drivers' education, DUI court, anger management classes, court-prescribed counseling, and so forth.
Financial	Refer to the legal actions above. All cost money, and it is not just money from the addicted person. Family members and people in close relationships are usually pulled into the financial loop. They are often more financially impoverished than the addicted person.

Job	Everyone involved becomes poor and unreliable employees (or employers), even though the family members are usually careful not to lose their jobs. During the later stages of the disease, the addicted person sometimes works steadily for only a few weeks or months at a time before another period of use with its associated problems and crises.
Health	Usually, family and significant others suffer stress-related health problems before the addicted person does. They often have accidents and chronic health problems. Late stage results for the addicted person include accidents, overdose, and organ damage.
Insanity or Death	These are the last two alternatives for both sides if help isn't sought.

Notes

- What stood out for you in this section?

- How will you make use of what you have learned?

Study Questions for the Addiction Chart

1. Put an X by the area that best describes where you are on the ladder. List your current problems in each area.

   __Family: _____
   __Social: _____
   __Legal: _____
   __Financial: _____
   __Job: _____
   __Health: _____
   __Insanity or death: _____

2. Do you see yourself going up or down the ladder?

   __Up
   __Down

3. Which of these
   family roles have
   you played?

   __Martyr/Saint
   __Savior/Hero
   __Clown (I can joke and be cheer-
      ful, so we won't have to face
      the situation)
   __Closed-down Person in Hiding
   __Problem Person (watch me do it
      worse)
   __Angry/Rageful Person
   __Worker Bee

   HINT: You have probably played all
   the roles, but you may find one that
   overrides all the others. That will be
   your "role" in times of crisis.

4. What roles have
   other family mem-
   bers played?

   _____
   _____
   _____

5. Starting with the
   step you see your-
   self on at the mo-
   ment, what changes
   can you make in
   order to start back
   up the ladder?

   _____
   _____
   _____

6. What is your most
   pressing problem at
   the moment? What
   first step can you
   make toward solv-
   ing it?

   _____

   _____

   _____

7. Who else has suf-
   fered problems
   due to your family's
   situation?

   _____

   _____

   _____

8. Will it be possible
   to share this infor-
   mation with others
   involved?

   _Yes
   _No

Notes

- What have you learned from these study questions?

- Who would you like to share this information with?

Planning an Informal Intervention

If you have the financial means to employ an interventionist, he/she will essentially follow the pattern presented here. A meeting will be arranged with you before the intervention to inform you of what to expect and what you can do to assist. If you have the financial means or insurance that will cover treatment, you can ask a facility that accepts your insurance or a treatment center of your choice to recommend an interventionist. They may have one on staff.

If you plan to do the intervention yourself, the following suggestions may be helpful, but whether the intervention is done by a professional or yourself, no outcomes are ever guaranteed. As you can see by our story, our intervention was initially met with scorn and anger. I thought it was a complete failure, but as time passed, we learned otherwise. There is no way to predict the outcome of any action, not even a well-planned intervention.

1. Unless you are a professional interventionist, do not ever try to talk to a person who is under the influence of any chemical.

It makes no more sense than trying to have a serious conversation with someone who is medicated for surgery. Wait until later.

2. Do not get the person out of any trouble that he or she may have gotten into while using chemicals. That is called "natural consequences." If you persist in getting the person out of his or her natural consequences or being supportive of anyone else doing the rescuing, nothing will be learned from the experience.

3. Your impulse may be to respond to chemical emergencies with anger or hurt. Try to keep in mind that you are dealing with a health issue and try to respond in that way. You both need a calm, clear, sober head in order to have any sort of productive interchange. Stay calm and rational. Decide on the following items for a time when an intervention is appropriate:

    • Where will the discussion/intervention take place?

    • Who will be present?

    • What specific facts or information will each person present? For instance, a child may say, "Dad, on my last birthday, you promised to take me out to dinner. I invited my best friend to go with us, and she came home from school with me. We waited, but you never showed up. She finally went home. You called later, and I heard Mom arguing with you because you had stopped in the bar on the way home.

Dad, please get help. I love you, and I want us to be a happy family."

4. Earlier in this book, you read what I decided to use as examples with my son. Many books have helpful suggestions on this subject. The main thing is to stick to the facts and recall specific incidents, with no emotional exaggerations, no criticism, and no judgments.

5. Practice saying what you want to say, maintaining a calm, even voice.

6. Always keep what you planned to say in your mind, Do not let yourself be manipulated into arguing, debating, or defending your actions, words, or motives. Do not allow yourself to be pulled off the subject at hand. If you let yourself get into a debate with a substance abuser, you lose!

7. Briefly describe how you and your family's lives are being affected.

8. Be prepared for excuses, accusations, promises, and attempts to make you feel like the guilty party. Just stay on the subject, and say what you planned to say.

9. Respond to suicide threats by putting the person in contact with a suicide prevention professional. Have crisis hotline numbers ready to hand to the person. Unless you are a trained suicide prevention specialist, you can only be supportive, supply

numbers, and call the police for help if the person attempts to harm himself or herself or others

10. Keep in mind that threats of suicide are often used by chemically dependent people to keep others hooked into their disease. It is the ultimate emotional blackmail. It is all right to openly discuss this threat and remind the person that, in the presence of alcohol or drug use (including some prescription drugs), it is often a physiological and emotional result of the chemicals and will pass. However, they will need some reassurance of these facts, so it is important that you have phone numbers handy that they can call and speak to a professional. Take any threats that include a time, place or intended suicide method very seriously.

11. After discussing the threat, continue with the intervention, if possible.

12. Do not fall into the old lectures, including questions, such as:

- Can't you see what you're doing to yourself?

- How could you do this to me? How could you do this to your mom? How could you do this to the kids? How could you do this to yourself?

- Don't you care about what you're doing to your health? Don't you care about what you're doing to your business? Don't you care about what you're doing to your future? Don't you care about what you're doing to your finances?

There is one answer to all those questions, and it is:, "When loss of control is the issue, you cannot talk, reason, threaten, or guilt the person back into control." It is lost! He or she *can't* care.

In reality, you can only decide what sort of life you want for yourself. Be prepared to state calmly the standards and limits for your *own* life and home. Take time to be sure you absolutely mean what you are saying. These cannot be vague hints or fantasyland wishes; they must be firmly thought-out standards and limits. They must be definite.

13. State consequences calmly and firmly. Once again, be rock-bottom certain that you will follow through or it will do more harm than good. The old "If you get drunk one more time, you're out of here" trick is a waste of breath when said on more than one occasion, or even acted on more than once. When you go back on your threat after being fed enough promises, you diminish your ability to be taken seriously. This time, do not say anything you are not absolutely certain you will act on and carry through with on a long-term basis. Be sure everyone involved in the intervention is united and committed to not wimping out if anger, crying, or threatening starts. Inability to stick to your guns when you're trying to save a life is not a sign of being a loving person. Sometimes, however, the person is ready for help and the intervention is a swift success. In such a case he or she may quickly agree to your demands and even express relief that it is "over."

14. Offer options for help. If you have the money to pay for treatment or insurance to cover it and have made arrangements with a treatment facility, offer that treatment at this time. We could never have afforded to offer free treatment to our son if my husband had not been working in the substance abuse field and had friends who were willing to provide treatment to a family member. If your loved one is not insured and does not have the money to pay for treatment, some wonderful treatment options are available for the asking. Find those sources in your area, make a list of them, and hand the list to the person at the end of the intervention. If he/she refuses for the moment, still hand them the list in hopes that he/she will make use of the resources at a later time. Be supportive of the person acting on any decision to get help immediately. But remember that the decision is theirs, not yours. It's their responsibility. And the outcome of the decision is not yours. It is the responsibility of the other person and will be between them and their Higher Power. As mentioned before, you can find many options to offer by calling the following offices:

- Your local Council on Alcoholism

- Local substance abuse treatment centers

- Local Mental Health Association

- Salvation Army

- Volunteers of America

- Alcoholics Anonymous

- Narcotics Anonymous

- Your state's agency on alcoholism and drug addiction

    These places should have a complete listing of treatment options for your area. They should also have lists of resources to meet different financial needs. In a perfect world, you might have an immediate treatment option ready and waiting. It is not necessarily your responsibility to put the person in treatment. You may want to simply hand them a list of options and allow them the experience of taking care of their own business. It will be helpful to express your support of whatever they do in the way of seeking help.

15. Immediately following the intervention, be prepared to act on your decisions regarding your own life, regardless of what the person intervened on decides to do. Hopefully, one of those decisions will be to take your home back as your own, and if the person is living in your home, you will already have their personal effects packed and ready to go. You will probably hear, "I guess I'll have to sleep in the streets." Not so. Most people have friends to stay with. If they don't, there are several choices for living arrangements, including the YMCA or the Salvation Army. However, where they go will be none of your business (remember the definition of "serenity"). Everyone in our society can find a place to go unless he or she chooses differently. (Many people do not take advantage of the options presented

to them because that housing would require them not to drink or use drugs, but that is not your business, either.) And don't fall for the "I don't have any transportation" heartwringer. Buses, friends, and taxis are available to anyone.

16. If you have not already attended at least six Al-Anon meetings, attend that many or more before attempting any sort of intervention. If you are attending Al-Anon, be sure to get a sponsor and work the twelve steps yourself. It can bring serenity, sanity, renewed self-acceptance, and a sense of direction and purpose back into your life.

Notes

- If you plan an intervention, write specific plans for it before proceeding.

- With or without an intervention, write a plan for how you want your life to continue from this day forward.

Helpful Shortcuts

The Three Cs
You didn't cause it.
You can't control it.
You can't cure it.
(You can only get on with your own life.)

The Three *Rs*
What is your responsibility?
What is their responsibility?
What is God's responsibility?

As mentioned, an interesting way to view the Three *Rs* is to look at yourself and your loved ones as if you were looking at the next-door neighbors and not someone who is personally involved with you. For instance, if the next-door neighbor's adult child were arrested for drunk driving, would you feel it was your responsibility to bail him or her out of jail? You would probably see it as a natural consequence of that person's actions. Therefore, it would be his or her responsibility, not yours. (It wouldn't be the responsibility of his/her family members either. Any person who drinks and drives needs to be responsible for handling their own consequences. Otherwise, how can they learn?) As you become more detached from the situation, you will start to see that most of your worries have been about outcomes. Trying to control outcomes is usually too big a job for you, and too big of a job for the other person as well. Often, outcomes are so big that they turn out to be God's responsibility. What a relief when you can let go of being responsible for other people and all the outcomes in their lives.

Look up the slogans in your Al-Anon literature. They are solid gold.

Self-Evaluation Questions

- Do you lose sleep because of a problem drinker/user?

- Do many of your thoughts revolve around the problem drinker/user?

- When asked about the substance abuser, are you less than honest about who he/she is now? Do you revert to how wonderful he/she used to be or how great things could be now, "if only"?

- Do you ask for promises about not drinking/using?

- Have you forgiven infidelities on the strength of flimsy excuses?

- Do you make threats or decisions and not follow through on them?

- Do you think everything would be all right if only the problem drinker/user would stop drinking/using?

- Are you starting to lose respect for him/her, as well as for yourself?

- Do you often feel frustrated, alone, fearful, or angry?

- Are you starting to doubt yourself or your abilities and wonder about your sanity? Are you unsure about whether you are being told truth or lies?

- Do you feel responsible for or guilty about the person's drinking/using behavior? Do you take the blame for situations even when you don't think you are truly to blame?

- Do you try to protect or conceal the actions of the problem drinker/user?

- Have you taken over many of the problem drinker/user's responsibilities?

- Do you try to exert tight control over household money?

- Do you usually go the extra mile (or more) to keep the peace?

- Do you feel the need to justify your actions and attitudes?

- Have you noticed physical symptoms in yourself, such as headache, a feeling of tightness in the stomach, stiff back/neck, sweating palms, indigestion, sleeplessness, or shakiness?

- Do you feel that nothing you can say or do will get through to the problem drinker/user? Do you believe that he/she cannot get better?

- Have you ever thought of calling the police because of the problem drinker/user's behavior?

- Have you ever thought of calling a friend or family member for assistance?

- Have you played detective, hoping to find evidence that you were right?

- Have you found drug paraphernalia among his/her belongings?

- Have you disposed of the alcohol, empty bottles, drugs, or medication that you found?

- Have you withdrawn from peers or family because of embarrassment or shame?

- Are the children in the problem drinker/user's home showing signs of emotional stress, such as crying, withdrawing, arguing, changing friends, having trouble in school, or rebelling?

- Is your personal relationship with the problem drinker/user starting to be affected by feelings of disgust?

- Have you allowed yourself to become involved in the substance abuser's legal, financial, or personal problems?

- Have you hoped that some person or situation would save them?

- Have you wanted to run away?

A yes answer to three or more of these questions indicates that you need to take a hard look at your role in the situation and make changes in your life that will produce a healthier life-style for you. Ironically, it will also be the most health-producing action for everyone else involved.

Notes

- Which of the questions most relate to you?

- Do you think a problem exists?

- What are you going to do about that?

.

If You Choose to Attend Al-Anon ...

- You will find Al-Anon listed in your phone book. Some newspapers list Al-Anon meetings.

- Attend at least six to eight meetings before passing any judgment on the program. If you do not feel the group is right for you, then try another one. You will eventually find a good fit.

- When you go, be an active listener. Listen for something that is helpful to you.

- Get a sponsor, even a temporary sponsor, even (heaven help us) a slightly imperfect one. Try not to pick the group saint. You'll see why as you grow in the program.

- Be sure your sponsor has worked the twelve steps. Study guides and pamphlets are available at Al-Anon meetings.

- If substance abuse in another person is not the present problem in your life, remember that you are still eligible for Al-Anon if you have had alcoholism, drug addiction, or any other addiction present in your life, in your family, in the workplace, or in a friend in the past or in the present. Does that leave anybody out?

• Most Al-Anon meetings will be listed as "open meetings." All who feel they can benefit from the program are welcome. A few meetings are closed to family members of alcoholics only, and such a limitation will be posted beside the meeting's name.

• All meetings operate in the same general way. A leader reads the opening statement. Everyone introduces himself/herself by first name only. The twelve steps are read. The topic for discussion is announced, and there may be readings from Al-Anon literature or there may be a guest speaker. People share in a general way how it was, what happened, and how it is now. People do not ask direct questions or give direct advice. There is no cross talk. The most potent benefits of the program can be yours simply by listening carefully and then asking someone (of the same sex as yourself) to be your sponsor after the meeting ends. They will tell you how to make an appointment to start working the twelve steps with them. A sponsor will only be of help to you if he/she has worked the steps. When you ask a person to be your sponsor, ask if they have worked the steps with a sponsor themselves. Don't be hurt if they politely refuse. It took me three tries to find my first sponsor. The first one I asked was ill, the second one was already sponsoring too many people (sponsoring can be very time-consuming), and the third one finally said yes.

Notes

- Where are the nearest and most conveniently timed meetings?

- Who are the people who most appeal to you as a potential sponsor?

- Who have you asked to sponsor you? Has that person worked the steps with a sponsor of their own?

- What are your plans to start working the steps with your sponsor?

Helpful Twelve-Step Concepts

- Get involved. Use the beginner's packet and other twelve-step literature. Carefully read the twelve steps, the twelve traditions, the Serenity Prayer, and slogans. If possible, attend meetings at least weekly or more often. Get a copy of the telephone list and people in your group. Don't be shy about calling people you meet there. Take on some chore for the group, such as making coffee, cleaning up, putting away chairs, or helping with the literature.

- Don't overwhelm yourself. Just try to live the program one day at a time.

- We do not come for another person. We come to help ourselves and share our experience, strength, and hope with others.

- We are experts only in our own stories. No one speaks for the group as a whole.

- There is no permanent group leader or "boss." All offices are revolving.

- We respect anonymity. No questions are asked. We aim for an atmosphere of love and acceptance.

- We do not judge, criticize, or argue. We do not give or ask for advice regarding personal or family affairs.

- Our group is not a sounding board for continually reviewing our miseries. We come to the meetings to learn a new way to detach ourselves from them. Part of our serenity comes from being able to live at peace with unresolved problems.

- When we have personal struggles that require more than our share of the group's time to explain, we save the details for our sponsor.

- We do not discuss other programs, therapies, philosophies, or counseling.

- We do not discuss religion, politics, national or international issues, or other belief systems or policies. As a group, we do not have any opinion on outside issues.

- Remember that the twelve-step program is a spiritual, not religious, program. It is open to people of all faiths as well as to people who choose to have no faith at all.

- We never suggest to another person what his or her concept of a Higher Power should be. The steps suggest only a belief in a power greater than ourselves, or "God as we understand Him."

- We utilize the program; we do not analyze it. It is not helpful to place labels on any degree of illness or health.

- Remember that each person is entitled to his or her opinions. He or she may express them within the precepts of each group. We are all equal. No one is more important than another.

- Remember that our sharing is only about how it was, what happened, and how it is now. We do not tell other people's stories or take their inventories. We do not crosstalk or use more than our share of the group's time. We strive to be good listeners. We do not try to control or manipulate the group.

- We do not bring or suggest literature, or other materials, that is not approved by Al-Anon.

Part of the beauty and wonder of the twelve-step programs is that at meetings we can say anything and know it stays there. Anything you hear at meetings, on the telephone, or from other members is confidential and not to be repeated to anyone, mates, family, relatives, friends, or even group members. In that way, the group remains a safe haven for all who attend.

Notes

- What job have you volunteered for or helped with at your meeting?

- In what way can you be of service to your group?

Journaling

During your journey of self-discovery, it will be very helpful to start keeping a journal and writing in it every evening before retiring.

Start with five compliments to yourself for that day. Don't be modest. Really compliment yourself. What do you like best about your personality, your looks, your abilities, and so forth? Be specific. For example, write, "I really like the fact that I am quiet but sincere and people enjoy talking with me."

Next, write at least five "gratitudes." There were those self-pity days when I couldn't seem to think of anything to be grateful for. My sponsor suggested I start my list with flush toilets, soap, and toothbrushes before working my way up from there. It never failed to give me the boost I needed in order to remember that, regardless of what was going wrong, an incredible lot was going right.

Note the high point of the day and the low point of the day, including a few comments on why each one came to mind when you were writing. Say a prayer for anyone you feel resentful toward. If you owe an amends, make a note to remind yourself of it for the next day.

If you are working the steps, make special note of anything you noticed during the day that pertained to the step you are working.

Note your part in anything uncomfortable that happened during the day and suggest to yourself a healthier way to handle *your* responses the next time you encounter such a situation.

List at least one "God wink," that is, something you would usually assume was a coincidence or piece of good luck. When you were a kid, maybe a favorite aunt would look at you across the room and give you a little wink. That wink said it all about how special you were and how much you were loved. God winks are the same thing. It is your Higher Power saying, "You are very special, and I love you."

Make a brief list of your plans for the following day. Be sure to include at least one item that is strictly for your own enjoyment.

A brief meditation before going to sleep could include the Serenity Prayer.

Upon arising the next morning, review your list for the day, paying special attention to the item you will be doing for your own enjoyment. If you are a praying person, you might want to start the day with a request that you be shown the will of the Higher Power and be given the strength to carry that out. Some people pray to be relieved of the bondage of self (ego), so they might be of better service to their fellow man.

Notes

- If you do not have a notebook for your journal, use this page to do your first evening's entry.

Five Compliments	1
	2
	3
	4
	5
Gratitudes	1
	2
	3
	4
	5
High Point	
Low Point	

Step Material	
Planning Future Healthier Responses	
God Winks	
Plans for Tomorrow	
Meditation or Prayer Before Sleep	

- As the weeks pass, read your past entries to look for patterns. You can learn a lot about yourself from your journal.

Expanded List of Characteristics
of Codependency

Denial

- Ignore problems/situations or pretend they aren't happening.

- Deny things are as bad as they really are, all the time watching them get worse.

- Tell yourself that things are getting better when you know that isn't true.

- Avoid thinking about solutions to your problems by staying busy, working too hard, spending too much money, or having periods of frantic action followed by periods of total inaction.

- Feel generally depressed and confused a great deal of the time.

- Suffer from stress-related or immune-suppressed illnesses.

- Have a fear of anger, criticism, blame, or falling short, and try at all cost to avoid such feelings.

- Find it easier to believe obvious lies than insist on the truth.

- Feel it is impossible to get to the truth.

- Have difficulty identifying your own feelings. Minimize or deny your feelings.

- Desire to see yourself as completely unselfish and dedicated to the well-being of others rather than see yourself as a person who is being lied to and used.

Dependency

- Become addicted to another person's potentials.

- Look for happiness and fulfillment outside yourself.

- Feel unable to love yourself. Feel incomplete without someone else to "complete" you.

- Wrap your life around someone else's, if possible. Lose your own identity in the name of loving someone else.

- Seek love and intimacy from people who are incapable of giving it.

- Worry you would be left alone if you could not totally meet the other person's needs.

- When asked how you are, start the response with how things are going with a loved one instead of how things are going with you.

- Feel you are the one person who can truly understand and help someone else.

- Become addicted to the cycle of crisis. Feel abandoned when you are not needed.

- If you were drowning, someone else's life would flash before your eyes. (That's a little joke.)

Caretaking and Controlling

- Feel responsible for other people's feelings, thoughts, actions, choices, wants, needs, well-being, and ultimate destiny. Become rigid and controlling.

- Believe people you care for are not capable of caring for themselves without your help or input. Think they couldn't make it without you.

- Feel anxiety, self-pity, guilt, and responsibility for helping with other people's problems.

- Feel compelled to help solve problems, such as offering unwanted advice, giving multiple suggestions, presenting multiple options, or offering a quick fix.

- Feel resentful or hurt when your help is not appreciated or acted on.

- Anticipate other people's needs. Wonder why others seldom do the same for you.

- Find yourself saying "yes" when you really want to say "no." Do things you do not really want to do. Do things others could, and should, be doing for themselves.

- Find that pleasing others is often more important than pleasing yourself.

- Find it easier to express outrage about wrongs done to others than wrongs done to you.

- Feel safest when you are giving. Feel uncomfortable when someone is giving to you.

- Find yourself attracted to needy people. Needy people with problems are attracted to you.

- Feel empty and useless if you do not have a crisis or problem to solve or someone to help.

- Change plans or drop what you are doing in order to help someone else.

- Overcommit yourself. Take on jobs you do not want to do.

- Attempt to convince others how they should behave, think, or feel.

- Lavish gifts and favors on those you care about, even if it stretches your budget.

- Use sex to gain approval and acceptance.

- Worry about outcomes in someone else's life, as though you could somehow control them.

- Use guilt and shame to manipulate others.

Low Self-Worth

- Much of your self-worth depends on being needed.

- Feel embarrassed and uncomfortable when you receive recognition, praise, compliments, or gifts.

- Are unable to ask others to meet your needs and wants.

- Value other people's approval over your own self-approval.

- Accept blame easily. Judge yourself harshly.

- Often feel uncared for.

- Get angry, defensive, self-righteous, or indignant when others blame and criticize you, yet constantly inwardly blame and criticize yourself.

- Feel different from others. Sometimes wonder why others see you as so normal on the outside when you feel so crazy on the inside.

- Take things personally. Often feel you are the target.

- May have been the victim of sexual/physical/emotional abuse, neglect, or abandonment.

- May have come from an alcohol- or drug-impaired home.

- Feel like a victim, even though many problems in your present life are the result of being a "volunteer."

- Have difficulty making decisions. Fearful of making mistakes.

- Often do not get things done to your own satisfaction.

- Feel guilt in many areas.

- Have had thoughts that life just isn't worth living.

- Try to help other people live their lives instead of living your own.

- Get artificial feelings of self-worth from being a helper or fixer to others.

- Feel embarrassed due to other people's failures and problems.

- Have lost hope that good things will ever happen to you or those you are trying to help/fix.

- Strive to prove you are worthy of being loved, but are willing to settle for being needed.

- Have difficulty saying "no."

- Constantly need to explain yourself and justify your actions.

- Are willing to accept unacceptable behavior in order to keep the peace.

- Fear losing the love of others if you cross them or make them angry in any way.

- Feel good about being seen as a saint/martyr. Receive many compliments from others who see you as able to bear up under impossible conditions.

Weak Boundaries/Compliance

- Compromise values and integrity to avoid rejection and other people's anger.

- Feel very sensitive to other's feelings. Take on the same feelings.

- Feel irrational loyalty. Remain in harmful or unhappy situations for too long.

- Place a higher value on others' opinions and feelings than your own.

- Fear expressing different opinions or feelings.

- Put aside personal interests and hobbies to do what others want. Try to "fit in" at all cost.

- Accept sex as a substitute for love.

- Say you will not tolerate certain behaviors from others but are unable to follow through.

- Make threats to leave but always give one more chance when pleaded with or threatened.

- When finally leaving bad relationships, enter into new ones that are equally bad.

- Allow others to hurt you emotionally, verbally, or physically.

- Accept obvious lies and excuses as reasons "why."

- Complain, blame, and try to control an unacceptable situation, but continue to accept abusive behavior.

- Make excuses for other people's unacceptable behavior.

- Unable to say "no" without following it with a lie or an excuse. Often unable to say "no" under any circumstances without feeling uncomfortable and guilty.

Obsession

- Experience chronic anxiety. May have been medicated for anxiety or depression.

- Spend an inordinate amount of time thinking about someone else.

- Lose sleep over problems and other people's behavior.

- Have chronic worry that won't let go of you.

- Have chronic low energy.

- Middle-of-the-night fears for others.

- Play detective and check on someone else.

- Abandon your own routine because you are so upset about someone or something else.

- Focus most, if not all, of your energy on another person's problems.

- Often unable to accomplish tasks or projects through to completion due to fragmented thinking or behavior.

- Often feel a crushing emotional weight that will not let go and immobilizes you.

- Sometimes feel gripped by an almost unbearable need to see, talk to, be near, or help the person you are obsessed with.

Anger

- Often express fear and hurt feelings as anger.

- Fear your own anger because it feels unmanageable.

- Feel frightened of other people's anger. Often have physical reactions such as a knot in stomach, sweating, instant headache, and so forth.

- Can be manipulated with anger.

- Inability to feel or express anger in healthy ways.

- Your frustration often leads to anger, which, in turn, leads to feelings of guilt and back to frustration. This can become a constant circle of feelings.

- Feel unable to be responsible for your own anger.

- Blame and punish others for "making" you angry.

- Repress feelings of anger, resulting in occasional violent temper outbursts.

- Do mean, petty, or cruel things to get even. Act hostile, or have tantrums.

- Repress anger. Exhibit it in depression.

- Place guilt and shame on yourself and others.

Lack of Trust

- Do not trust yourself.

- Do not trust your feelings.

- Do not trust your decisions.

- Do not trust other people

- Feel abandoned, even by your Higher Power.

Poor Communication

- Often do not say what you mean or mean what you say.

- Feel frustrated and irritable when trying to explain feelings and thoughts.

- Try to say what will be pleasing to other people.

- Talk about other people's problems, feelings, and actions but seldom discuss your own personal feelings and actions.

- Place blame and guilt when feeling threatened.

- Lie to protect and cover for people you love.

- Lie to protect yourself from embarrassment or humiliation due to your present situation.

- Have difficulty verbally asserting your rights.

- Have difficulty expressing emotions honestly, clearly, and calmly.

- Blame and call other people names during arguments.

- Bring up old resentments in new situations.

- Do not employ fair fighting techniques.

- Cry or rage to avoid communicating with words.

- Have poor listening skills.

- Stonewall communication in order to stop uncomfortable discussion or control the situation.

- Have difficulty getting to the point.

- Learn to gauge words carefully in order to manipulate the desired results.

- Either cannot say "no" or only feel safe and in control by saying "no" to everything.

- Unable to find middle ground between never saying "no" or always saying "no." Feel trapped in your own pattern.

- Rapidly changing emotions make it difficult to communicate calm, clear messages.

- Not always able to think rationally because feelings get in the way.

- Communicate confusion to everyone around you.

- Often feel impatient with people who need your undivided attention, even your children.

Health Issues

- Have a chronic, stress-related illness.

- Have tense muscles, stiff neck, or back problems

- Have digestive problems.

- Suffer from insomnia or other sleep disturbances. Sleep too much or too little.

- Chronically fatigued.

- Are prone to accidents due to muddled thinking or constant worry.

Look back at the areas you have checked off. You will see a pattern. That pattern will give you a starting point for working the twelve steps with a sponsor. It will also give you an overview of where you are in your personal growth. Note anything that strikes you as an area you can work on in order to make your life richer and more fulfilling. Be gentle with yourself and forgiving. Every human being on earth is in the learning process. This is just one tool to help you on your way.

Notes

- What three areas can you start to work on right now?

- What changes will be you striving for?

About the Author

B arbara F. was a special education teacher and resource specialist during the early part of her son's alcoholism and drug addiction. In time, her son's addictions changed her focus to the field of substance abuse rehabilitation. At that time, her husband, Bob, was director of Operation Cork, a foundation funded by the Kroc family, who contributed generously to the substance abuse recovery field. Together, Bob and Barbara opened and operated their own substance abuse treatment center, one of the early pioneers of host living inpatient treatment. Barbara specialized in family issues. She later worked for the state of Texas as a licensure and compliance officer, working with substance abuse treatment centers and in-prison programs in the southern half of that state. Most recently, they completed four years on the island of Maui, working as substance abuse counselors, where Barbara continued to specialize in family issues.

Bob and Barbara presently live in Tucson, Arizona, where both continue to work in the substance abuse recovery field.

Barbara also does personal coaching and education for people who are dealing with addiction issues within the family or in other personal relationships.

Anyone who would like contact Barbara or contribute their personal story of encouragement to be included in an upcoming book on the miracles of family recovery may contact her at:

Barbara F.

PMB 252

6336 N. Oracle Rd., Suite #326

Tucson, AZ 85704

or

Barbfamhealing@wmconnect.com

Robertbarb888@msn.com

Printed in the United States
68183LVS00003B/364-441